Lara Bernardi

BERNARDI Profile

The Keys to Your Personal and Professional Success

Foreword
Martin Zoller

novum pro

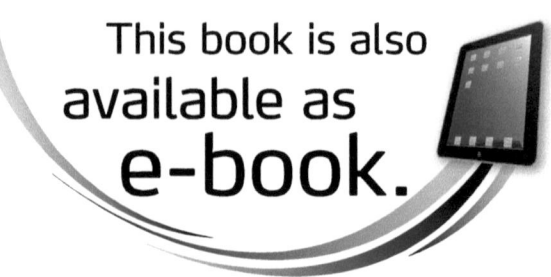

www.novum-publishing.co.uk

All rights of distribution, including via film, radio, and television, photomechanical reproduction, audio storage media, electronic data storage media, and the reprinting of portions of text, are reserved

Printed in the European Union on environmentally friendly, chlorine- and acid-free paper.

© 2016 novum publishing

ISBN 978-3-99048-618-4
Cover photo: Lara Bernardi
Cover design, layout & typesetting: novum publishing
Internal illustrations: Lara Bernardi (37)

www.novum-publishing.co.uk

This book is dedicated to my three "treasures" Luana, Mia, and Aira. I love you and thank you for everything.

Love,
Lara

TABLE OF CONTENTS

Foreword 9

Introduction 12
   Holistic Model of Personality 14
   Consciousness – Sub-consciousness –
   Super-consciousness 17
   Prerequisites for Success 21

Who Am I? 33
   Tree – Recognize your potential 34
   Inner Team – Identify your Personality Type 48
   The Inner Team 51
   Tree Meditation: Connecting Above and Below 58

Where Am I now? 60
   Colors – Become Aware of
   Your Personal Attributes 61
   Cycles – Recognize Your Personal Rhythm 80
   Chakras – Recognize Your Energy Levels 96
   Rainbow Breathing – Create Personal Balance 109

What is my Mission? 111
   Heart Meditation –
   Strengthen Your Personal Center 112
   Relationship Map –
   Get to Know Your Inner Map 114
   Shamanic Timeline Journey –
   Mission Made Conscious 123

What Are My Visions? 130
    Project Management – Course of Action
    to Realize Personal Goals 131
    Find Your Vision –
    Develop Your Motivational Phrase 141
    Seeking Your Vision – Develop a Vision
    for all Aspects of Your Life 146
    Goal Programming – Begin Realization 150

What else can I let go of? 152
    Energies – Summon Up Strength for Action 154
    Reflection – Keep it Going 162
    Releasing Ritual – Release the Final Baggage 163

Closing Remarks 164

Lara Bernardi 165

FOREWORD

The coming years are years of change that will offer mankind the opportunity to grow and develop very quickly. If you actively use this time, you can accomplish much. Moreover, you will generate strength and motivation for the challenges of daily life. But actively engaging in this process does not mean that you have to run at high speed. Take time for quiet and rest. Leave daily worries behind and let your soul soar. Enjoy these flights.

All of the challenges that lie ahead should be seen as opportunities to grow and move forward. Say "yes" to what is. Everything happens for a reason. Nothing in the universe happens by chance.

If you are sensitive and open, you will perceive the moods of the world and of Mother Earth. If you are conscious of this, you will realize that you can let go of what is not yours. And it is worthwhile to learn to be present in yourself. If you do this, you will be able to better handle the buffetings of life. You will not be so easily excited. You will no longer be drawn to resonate with things external and will not be so absorbed by them. You will only resonate with situations that have to do with you or that offer you a chance to grow. Accept this opportunity. Go forward and create a worthwhile life. We are all children of Mother Earth. Care for her and your environment. Love, respect, humility, thankfulness, and trust will bring you and others forward.

Connect with nature – trees, stones, and the heavens. They will strengthen your aura, the invisible space around your physical body. Take flights of fancy. Open yourself to the heavens above you by appreciating the starry sky or filling up on sunlight.

Centering your heart chakra through a heart meditation will bring you inner peace and tranquility.

Visit these places regularly and enjoy the all-encompassing love that you feel with in. This love is a beautiful companion for the path that stands before you. Choose consciously. Be brave. I wish you strength, love, and success. Light and love shall stream through you and be with you on your way.

Love,
Lara

The culmination of every person is the realization of their talents and mission! Who wouldn't like to feel and know their life's mission?

Although we carry many answers as to our life's path within, it is often difficult to find them. Usually this is not because we lack the connection, but because we have no entry to our inner self! Something that could be very simple often becomes a long and complicated search.

I have known Lara Bernardi for many years and am impressed by her knowledge and ability. She can help people progress on the holistic path of the soul with her experience.
Thanks to her insightful work, she helps her fellow man ask the right questions so that they can receive the right answers.

Thanks to the intuition that we all carry within, we can create a spiritual map for our life's path. Meditations and exercises like those in this book are a wonderful support to create these plans.

All paths lead to Rome and the better the map, the clearer and more defined the journey. You don't need magic or superhuman powers to connect with your soul's essence. This is another wonderful conclusion that readers of this book will realize.

"If she could do it, so can I!" This will be the reaction of everyone who reads this book. And it's true! There are many people like Lara and myself and there are also many different techniques to follow the soul's journey. What is important is that you feel good and satisfied on your journey.

Thanks to this book, you, dear reader, will feel good and validated that you chose to follow the path of self-awareness and personal growth!

I wish you many relaxed and memorable moments with this book and on your life's journey!

Sincerely,
Martin Zoller,
www.martinzoller.com

INTRODUCTION

Since time immemorial, people have asked themselves: Who am I? What can I accomplish? Where is it all leading? Images within, our inner voice, and our feelings are paths to self-knowledge and inspiration. Even Goethe said: "Do you wish to roam farther and farther? See the good that lies so near." The happiness and sometimes unfathomable potential of every human being lie within us. Our exterior reflects only what a person thinks and feels. The true treasure lies within, in the heart chakra of every human being.

Personal and professional success depends on how far you manage to identify and understand yourself. Do you know who you are, what you are capable of, and where you want to go? Clarifying these questions will bring you stability, security, and understanding in these current, mercurial times. They also increase your self-confidence and self-awareness. Self-knowledge is the key to your potential and to personal and professional success. When we truly know ourselves, we can better understand ourselves and others and also better handle what life brings us.

Because mankind is striving to find the right path, there is now a great demand for personality and aptitude tests, as well as books on these topics. Accordingly, the market is flooded with a variety of tests. Each method measures something different and yet often the same – and *all* of them promise the key to success. In this jungle, it is not easy to find the right tool or the right path for personal development. When choosing the appropriate method, it is important that the chosen tool matches your personal goals, attitudes, and values. Moreover, it is worthwhile to explore new paths and to choose a holistic approach that captures the personality as a whole. The subject must learn to let go of the old; change and development are only possible in this way.

This book is a guide for your personal and professional success. Based on personality and aptitude tests as well as meditations, you will find answers to the questions: Who am I? What is my current reality? What is my mission? Which visions guide me? What can I release?

The personality and aptitude tests in this book are part of the BERNARDI Profile®. It is based on theories of C. G. Jung, teachings of colors and symbols, and knowledge of Indigenous Peoples. The profile provides a bridge from analytical to creative thinking and the so-called "soft skills" (i.e., social skills). It supports you in recognizing your personality, helping you to develop your own potential and to be successful. The profile includes a variety of innovative exercises and meditations. These help you dive deep, and highlight unconscious themes and aspects of your personality. Thus, you get to know and understand your personality better. You will gain security and stability, and can better deal with growing professional and personal demands. You strengthen your center, and increase your satisfaction, serenity, and motivation in your professional and personal life.

The approach presented in this book addresses the personality as a whole. This holistic view of your personality is symbolized by the five elements. Earth, water, fire, and air are integral elements in the formation of the earth. The fifth element, ether, is called "pure love" in the movie of the same name. It embodies the abstract, the regions that are unconscious and invisible. The holistic approach and integration of personal and professional topics increases your awareness. Awareness is the first step to greater satisfaction, happiness, joy, and love in your life.

Holistic Model of Personality

The holistic view of personality is the key to success and provides answers to many unanswered questions. The personality includes the physical body, the emotions, the "Inner Fire", the mind, and the spirit. Four of the five levels (body, emotions, mind, and spirit) are referred to as man's "Inner Team". The fifth level, the "Inner Fire", synthesizes the other four. A person who acts from his center, from his "Inner Fire", is a holistic person. Such types are intrinsic entrepreneurs, healers, teachers, and coaches and are inherently holistic.

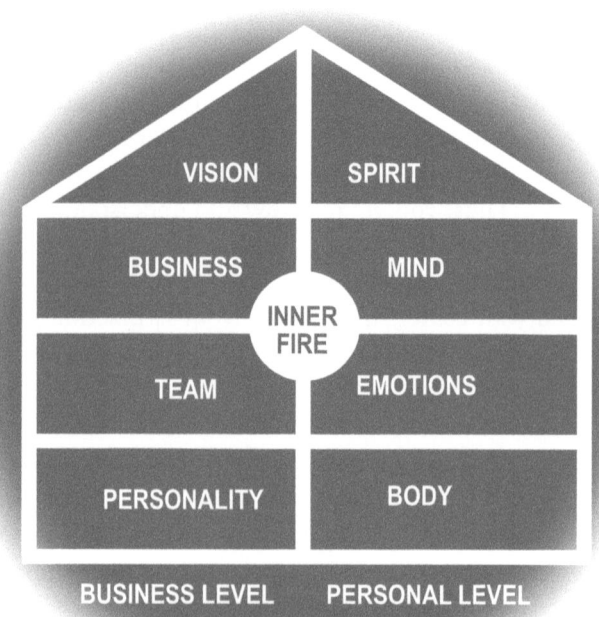

A holistic worldview is self-contained. The same themes show up with different names and forms on different planes. The same laws rule on all planes. Other principles are the five elements: Earth, water, fire, air, and ether. They are explained in the chapter on project management in this book.

The five levels of personality are associated with different characteristics:
- **Physical Body (Perceiver)** This is the material body of a person with its organs, cells, and constitution. This part of your body processes facts and information arriving through the five senses.
- **Emotional Body (Sensor)** This part of your body senses, saves, and processes emotions. A socially competent person consciously receives the information that flows in through this body. Thus, he can sense what others are feeling and better understand their actions and behavior.
- **The "Inner Fire" (Entrepreneur, Healer, Teacher, Coach)** This level is the symbolic representation of application, the power of inspiration, and the inner wisdom of humanity. The "Inner Fire" is your personal center. When you are completely focused in the present moment, you are fully anchored in your center. On the physical level, the "Inner Fire" is associated with the heart.
- **The Mental Body (Thinker)** This level analyzes, plans, and saves thoughts. Specialized knowledge is retained here. This is the "heady" side of a person. Students and managers are especially active at this level in their daily life.
- **The Spiritual Body (Intuitive)** Here, creative inspiration and innovative ideas spring forth. Philosophers and inventors such as Pythagoras and Albert Einstein drew their wisdom and teachings from this level. These insights are sometimes called "gut feelings". Insights appear as sudden inspirations or images. Because these insights are not rationally comprehensible, many people do not trust their intuition.

The areas: Body, emotions, "Inner Fire", mind, and spirit can also be translated to the business world. Here, they have different names: Personality, team, "Inner Fire", business, and vision. Another name for "Inner Fire" is values. The same themes show up with different names and forms, following the same principles.

The five levels of personality also characterize a person's charisma. They are the person's sun and are influenced by what a person thinks, feels, and how he acts. A civil servant, for example, who operates on the material plane, has a different energy than a scientist, who works on the mental plane. Our charisma is also dependent on our daily state of mind. The more positive a person is, the more he shines.

A charismatic personality has a powerful radiance that enthralls and engages others. If a person isn't feeling well, he can hardly enthuse others. Negative thoughts also dull our gleam. It certainly holds true: "Birds of a feather flock together." Positive thinking is the cure at all levels of the personality.

Consciousness – Sub-consciousness – Super-consciousness

According to brain research, the subconscious comprises 90% of human consciousness. In communication with other people, sub-conscious messages also comprise around 90% of the information transmitted. Everything that we perceive concretely in our everyday life with our mind and five senses is part of the consciousness, which makes up the other 10%. That means that the spoken word, for example, corresponds to only 10% of what the recipient receives.

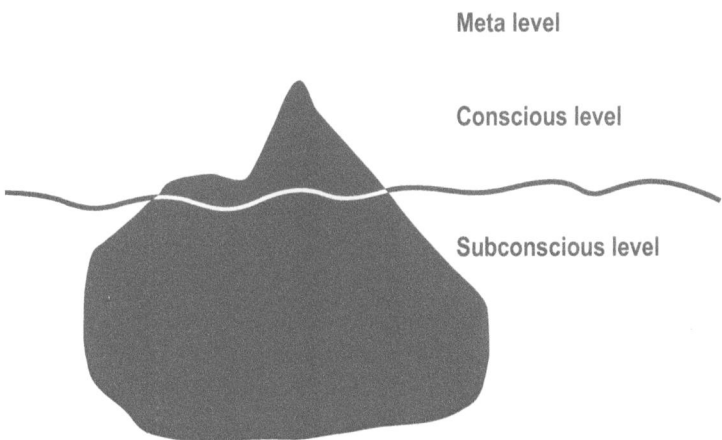

A person's beliefs, unconscious behavior patterns, blockages, and suppressed emotions are stored in their subconscious. The subconscious lies deep within. Its language is symbols and images, which are often not understood by the person concerned. Dreams also reveal subconscious themes.

The subconscious also serves a protective function for human consciousness. It works like a funnel. The more conscious information one receives, e.g., articles or news reports, the faster information seeps in from the conscious into the subconscious. Automatic behaviors also belong to this category. A typical automatic behavior is driving. Many people who have been driving for a long time turn, change gears, and brake automatically without thinking. But this smooth driving had to be trained. Things don't usually go so smoothly during the first hours of driving. The same is true for all other actions in life. The more a person does something, the more automatic it becomes. This includes, for example, reaching for the morning cup of coffee. Our first actions when we get to work in the morning are also mostly automatic.

The unconscious effect of brands on consumers also shows how much people are dominated and controlled by unconscious influences. People buy Coca-Cola and Nivea instead of rival brands because of the brand. The brands convey emotions that speak to and control the consumer's subconscious mind. Interestingly, Coke always performs more poorly than competitors in blind taste tests. (Note: In blind tests, the subjects try the products without knowing what they are drinking.) If the test subjects know what they are drinking, however, Coke scores better than the other products. This pattern from market research is an example of the power of the subconscious mind. Man uses his brain predominantly for data storage; but he should use it even better, as Albert Einstein suggested.

A plane that is often neglected in both practice and literature is the super-conscious, the meta level. It is the bird's eye view, from which you can look at situations and things from a neutral position. This perspective supports a neutral, value-free, holistic perspective. It is a state of consciousness independent of space and time, in which limiting belief systems and behavior patterns are turned off. Through this expanded scope, processes and interactions are made visible in their entirety. Not-yet conscious causes of fears, blockages, and behaviors are recognized.

EXERCISE: Gain objectivity with a bird's eye view

1. Take time for a few quiet minutes. Turn off your cell phone and other sources of interruption. Breathe deeply in and out through your nose. Concentrate on deep, abdominal breathing.
2. When you have relaxed a bit, take three sheets of paper. Title one "sub-conscious", the second "conscious", and the third "super-conscious". Place these three sheets of paper like a path before you on the floor. "Sub-conscious" should be directly in front of your feet. The next sheet is "conscious" and the furthest sheet "super-conscious".
3. Focus on the issue about which you wish to achieve clarity. Possible topics include: Clarity in your partnership, the cause of a conflict, or what the next step in a particular situation should look like.
4. Step onto the sheet labeled "sub-conscious", close your eyes, and take a few deep breaths. Wait and see what ideas (inspiration) come into your mind regarding your issue. Note: These intuitive ideas will come as mental images, or flashes of thoughts or feelings. Let yourself be surprised.
5. Before you move onto the sheets "conscious" and "super-conscious", return to the starting position, a.k.a. the neutral position. Concentrate again on your issue and then stand on the sheet "conscious". Close your eyes and take a few deep breaths. Wait and see what ideas (inspiration) come into your mind regarding your issue.
6. Return to the starting position once again. Focus on your issue and then stand on the sheet "super-conscious". Close your eyes and take a few deep breaths. Wait and see what ideas (inspiration) come into your mind regarding your issue.
7. Write down your insights when you are done.

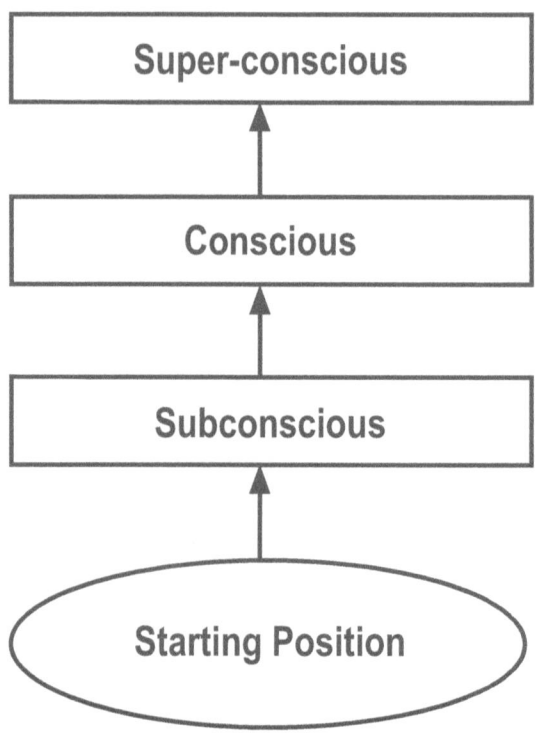

Prerequisites for Success

More and more people feel the desire to break out from the boundaries of their lives. This requires that they expand their personal limits and thought-horizon. Moreover, old and outdated ideas, beliefs, and behavior patterns must be released, so that there is room for the new. The principle of Feng Shui says that overstuffed wardrobes must first be cleared out before new clothes can have space. Order brings clarity. Break and rest periods are necessary. They help you to evaluate and organize your characteristic actions and thoughts. It is very worthwhile to consciously examine yourself from time to time.

Instructions for Personal Success

1. Recognize and understand your personality using self-tests and meditations
2. Determine your personal and professional goals
3. Develop your potential with the help of personal actions
4. Secure your long-term success through endurance and patience.

Success is what succeeds, i.e., it succeeds (comes from) an earlier action. Success can therefore only occur when a person sets goals and then aims with all their strength to accomplish them. One of the most important conditions for success is one's own will. Additionally, it is crucial whether or not these goals and desires come from the heart. A first step towards coming closer to our heart's desire is to recognize our personal values. Once you have identified them, you can match them with your goals. Values come from the personal center of a person. They come from the heart.

EXERCISE: Identify your values

Everyone is looking for something different. Some people want a lot of money and luxury, i.e., material success, while others value intangibles. Values are motivators. They give strength as we strive to realize our personal goals. The more conscious you are of your values, the more easily you will get what you want. Your heart's desires are the strongest power in the universe. They radiate with powerful energy and draw your desires like a magnet into your life.

What are your three top values? Cross out the values in the following list that are less important to you. In the end, only three values should remain. Prioritize the remaining three values in order of importance. Of course, you can also personalize and expand the list.

List of Values:
- Respect/Deference
- Discipline
- Honesty
- Freedom
- Equality/Fairness/Justice
- Happiness
- Harmony
- Identity
- Skill/Competency
- Love
- Power
- Openness
- Order
- Punctuality
- Cleanliness
- Tolerance
- Faithfulness/Fidelity/Loyalty
- Trustworthiness
- Peace

From now on, when you set a goal for yourself and strive to accomplish something, check whether or not it is in harmony with your values.

EXERCISE: Clean-up negative thoughts and outdated beliefs

According to quantum research, you create your own life and reality. What you believe becomes your reality. That is why it is so important to release old and outdated thoughts and beliefs.

It is not always easy to recognize negative thoughts and outdated beliefs. It is therefore recommended to perform this exercise with a trusted person or coach, or to consider your own thoughts from a bird's eye perspective.

Think about what goes on in your head every day. What do you think about yourself, about your life, and about the opportunities in your life? Do you believe that everything in your life could be easier and simpler? Do you believe in a positive future?

In the left column, write down all your negative thoughts and beliefs. Then in the right column, write down positive thoughts and beliefs. Write sentences that motivate you and that are formulated positively.

-	+
Example I can't change anything in my current situation. I would like to reduce my job from 100 to 80%, but my boss/the company won't let me. I don't have any time left for me personally after my job and my family. My family doesn't understand what I want. They don't understand me.	Example I am lord and master of my life and hold the reins in my hand. I stand up for my wishes and needs, so that I get what is important for me. Starting today, I will create free time for myself. I think very carefully about what I want and what is important to me. I then share this clearly. I pay attention to my feelings in my conduct. I am transparent about my reactions to situations and share my needs with others.

EXERCISE: Work-Life Balance

Work-life balance means the reconciliation of work, private, and family life. In a broader sense, this term includes the desire to achieve a sense of balance and personal centeredness. Whoever dwells entirely in their center is quiet and relaxed. A centered person observes life with equanimity and can accept events and others as they are.

He who lives the principle, "as within, so without", finds peace. This means that the external circumstances must correspond to your inner desires. That is why it is crucial to recognize what is important to you and where you want to invest more time and energy.

A first step to a fulfilling and satisfying work-life balance is the time that you take for things important to you. Personal development, through coaching, seminars, books, meditation, and personality analysis, for example, support you in recognizing the important things in your life.

Procedure:
1. Draw a pie chart of your day. Assume a 16-hour day, excluding the hours that you are asleep. How much time do the various sectors take up during a normal working day?
   Possible sector divisions:
   - Work
   - Education
   - Partner
   - Family/Children

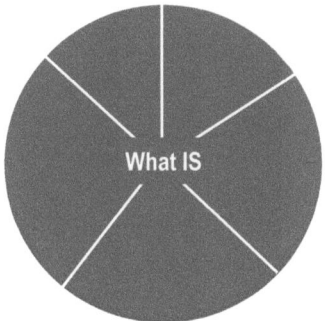

   - Free time
   - Hobbies
   - Friends
   - Etc.

2. Recognize your "stressors", i.e., anything that is stressing you. Look at your present situation and ask yourself the following questions:
   - Where are my stressors?
   - Are certain sectors especially stressing?

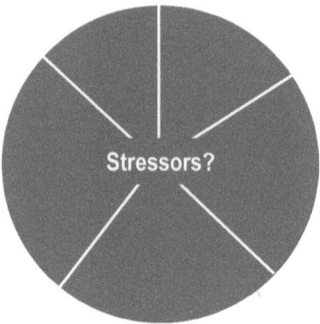

3. What would your ideal work-life balance look like? Draw a new pie chart based on this ideal, without looking at the actual situation. Reach for the stars and allow yourself to imagine impossible things. Your ideal *must* be visionary! It is important that it motivates and inspires you to further develop your life. Dare to move forward and to re-create your life in a way that feels right for you. Some changes take time. Surely you can find ways to take immediate action, making you happier and more satisfied.

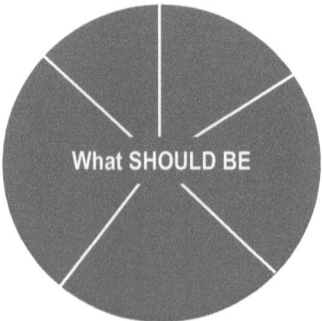

There is no perfect example of work-life balance. Everyone has different needs and desires. In practice, however, many people spend too much time on their jobs and too little time on their own needs and hobbies. Relaxation, calm, and moments of reflection are important for every person. You can and should make more time and space in your life for the things that are important to you, the things that are dear to your heart.

Whatever time remains after work is spent with family and partner. Even friends have little place in this picture. As long as family and partner bring fulfillment and energize with strength and new motivation, there's nothing wrong with this. It becomes difficult, however, when family and partner are a burden. What good is a demotivated father who is always mentally absent during an outing with the children? What good is a mother who is burned out and unhappy? Everyone benefits from quality times spent together. There are more opportunities for time together or a few quiet moments alone when annoying familial responsibilities and other invitations, only fulfilled out of obligation, are kept to a minimum. It is worth it to say "no". Your loved ones, and you yourself, will thank you for it. Every "no" makes room for a "yes".

4. Finally, develop personal habits that will support your move from your current to your ideal work-life balance. The habits should be simply and easily applicable.
5. Prioritize your habits and begin working towards your top priority today.
6. Finally, ask yourself the following questions (just before bed is a good time):
    - What do I notice about my work-life balance?
    - What are my personal goals pertaining to work-life balance?
    - When I compare my current and my ideal balance, what will I change starting today?
    - What areas of my life need more time – starting today?
    - Which "dream" ideas can actually be achieved?

- What habits/conditions will support me in reaching my ideal balance?
- How will I handle stressors? What are some possible solutions?

TIP: Find inner peace

An important part of achieving inner peace is work-life balance. Work-life balance begins in each person. The term work-life balance is misleading, however. It separates work from life, yet conveys beautifully the image of a scale. On one side are the personal needs and time that every person has available outside our professional activities. The other side of the scale is filled with work.

This is how you can find inner peace:
1. Be thankful for what you have and what you are.
2. Allow every being to be themselves and some things to just be.
3. Give every being space while fully inhabiting your own space.
4. Practice patience and understanding for yourself and others.
5. Value yourself.
6. Trust yourself and your personal and professional future.
7. Do something every day that brings you joy.
8. Find joy in what you do; celebrate your personal successes.
9. Complete unpleasant tasks quickly.
10. Focus on things and people who motivate you and do you good.
11. Schedule time for relaxation at least once/day (quality, not quantity makes the difference here).
12. Schedule a set time every week for quiet moments/free time to think about your visions and new ideas for the future.
13. Write down your visions and goals, and how you want to achieve them.
14. Concentrate your strength and energy on personal and professional visions and goals.
15. Believe that you can achieve these goals.
16. Be steadfast in your pursuit of your goals.
17. Be flexible, not narrow-minded.

EXERCISE: Plan your future success

Take a few minutes and think about your personal and professional goals. Set specific goals. What do you want your life to look like in one year? In five years? For your motivation, it is also important how you formulate these goals. Bear in mind:

Your goals should be
- motivating,
- realistic,
- specific and positive.

Possible examples could be: As of 1.1.2014, I will earn $10,000/month; or, starting today, I will interact with my boss and partner with self-confidence and certainty.

	My one-year goals	My five-year goals
Personally		
Professionally		
Other		

You need courage, strength, and endurance to reach your goals. One way to tank up on energy is gratitude. This releases a lot of power that you can use for new projects. Every step forward requires energy. Practice gratitude for everything that you have already received or achieved. You can also be grateful for that which is to come. You will see how good it feels (see: Exercise: Gratitude).

Tip: Energetic Methods

What indigenous peoples know is also helpful for western people. One principle is: If you want to evolve, you need energy. Even Chinese medicine assumes that disease results from a blockage of energy in the body. Energetic methods help the energy to flow and unlock strength for the next steps. Moreover, blockages that prevent a person from moving through their life in a relaxed and detached manner are released.

Energetic work also includes transmitting strength through the laying on of hands. The coach places his hands on the client's body at the right time and in the right place. The client perceives the energy flowing through the coach's hands into his body as a pleasant warmth. Hands symbolize action. By laying on of hands, blockages and heaviness can be released. Furthermore, power for the next steps is transfused.

It is really worthwhile to receive an energetic treatment from an experienced professional whenever you feel an inner need for calm and recovery, or if you just want to do something good for yourself.

EXERCISE: Thankfulness

In a quiet moment, think about what you are thankful for in your life. What can you be really proud of? What have you already achieved? Bow your head and give voice to your gratitude, silently or aloud.

Bowing conveys humility. The spiritual world will feel motivated to continue to support you and stand by your side. Consciously feel your gratitude in the center of your chest in your heart chakra. Perhaps you also have a different place in your body that transmits the feeling of gratitude.

From this moment on, practice gratitude whenever you have achieved something or you get something unexpected. You can always practice gratitude, if you want to recharge your personal strength.

Instructions for successful completion of the self-tests

The following self-tests from the BERNARDI Profile® will support you in achieving personal and professional success. The tests use the language of the subconscious mind, i.e., they are based mainly on symbols and colors. The analytical mind will have difficulty understanding this process. The advantage of this is that the results cannot be manipulated. They are therefore genuine.

Procedure:
1. Approach the tests with an easy, relaxed attitude.
2. Allow enough time for the tests. You can take a test once a week or every other week, for example, and apply the appropriate tips and exercises in the intervening time.
3. Listen to your intuition as you take the tests, which can speak to you in the form of an inner voice, images, or feelings. Observe your first impulse as you take the tests. The longer you

wait, the more likely your rational brain will take over. Your intuition will give you an answer within a few seconds. This is not only the case in these exercises! Your intuition is that fast in everyday life, as well.
4. Only read the results of the self-tests *after* you have completed them.
5. Read the results and ask yourself each time, what they actually mean for you. What conclusions do you draw from the exercise?
6. In case you want to look at some of the exercises with me or a trained BERNARDI Profile® Coach, you can contact me through my website: www.bernardi.li.

WHO AM I?

Do you know who you are, what you can do, and where you want to go? Using these personality and aptitude tests and meditations you will find the answers to your questions: Who Am I? What is my personal and professional potential? Self-knowledge is the key to your potential and thus to your personal and professional success. You gain strength and motivation. Furthermore, you will recognize your blockages and find the keys to the solutions. The first step is your consciousness. Then you can decide if you want to continue your self-work alone. Perhaps you will feel an inner impulse telling you that you should accept outside help from an experienced coach. Listen to yourself. You carry the answers within you. Your heart awareness/intelligence always has an answer and already provides possible solutions.

Tree – Recognize your potential

The language of the sub-consciousness is colors, symbols, and images. One way to make contact with your subconscious is to examine your dreams. Indians say that unread dreams are like unread letters. They contain important messages that are often not recognized and respected in everyday consciousness. Other ways to get in touch with your unconscious aspects are through meditation and drawing. In meditation, we fall into the alpha state where both right and left brain are active. This gives the meditator access to his intuition, which is in direct contact with the subconscious. It is the conduit to the subconscious areas of life. Drawings also show unconscious images. You can learn more about yourself by drawing. The tree drawing provides information about your personality. It reveals your tapped and untapped potential. The tree is symbolic of your personality.

Self-test: Tree

Complete the exercise as follows:
- Take a box of colored pencils and a blank piece of paper. If you don't have any colored pencils handy, you may use a regular pencil or a pen.
- Draw your tree on the paper spontaneously. Draw it as it appears to you. Let yourself be led and let go of all thoughts as long as you are drawing. Don't judge or evaluate. It does not have to be a masterpiece. Draw your tree with all that that entails for you. Forget everything you have heard so far about tree drawings and tree analysis. Go with the flow while drawing.
- When you are finished, look at your drawing and ask yourself if something is missing. If yes, add it to your drawing.

Classical Tree Analysis

After you have drawn your tree, as a first step compare your tree with the various points of the classical tree analysis. This analysis is also used in psychological testing methods.

To assess your drawing, use the graphic of the classical tree analysis in combination with the following questions. Consider the answers to the following questions in relation to your person. You will see your impact and your themes more clearly:
1. What do I notice in my drawing and in my tree?
2. Is my tree full-grown or is it still growing? How big could it grow? The full-grown size of your tree shows your potential. The tree can also grow beyond the edges of the paper.
3. How big is your tree? Does it have enough room on this piece of paper? The size of your tree shows you how much room you make for yourself in your life and who much room you need to develop and feel good. Great trees indicate great potential.
4. Does your tree have roots? The roots show whether or not your feet are firmly planted on the ground.
5. Is your trunk stable or flexible? Imagine that a powerful wind comes. Does your tree bend with the wind? The tree's flexibility indicates your flexibility in life.
6. Does your tree bear fruit? Fruit stands for the things you can harvest. Think about what you can harvest in your life. What can you be proud of? Label your fruit with these things. Your harvest could be professional or personal abilities and experiences that you are proud of. Each fruit should be labeled with an ability or an experience when you are done. You can ask trusted people close to you for their ideas and input.
7. Does your tree have leaves? Is the transition from trunk to crown protected? Leaves are like a protective sheath. They represent protection. If your center (the transition from trunk to crown) is without leaves, this indicates elevated sensitivity and vulnerability.
8. Is your tree located in the future (right side of the paper) or in the past (left side)? If your tree is in the middle of the paper, you are living in the "now". You are living in the present moment. If your tree is in the past, it shows that you still need to release old themes. When you no longer talk about or think about old issues, then you are free for a new future.

"Chakra Tree of Life"

The tree can also be understood on a higher level. In so doing, you can identify your personal blockages and potential for development. The model with the seven main chakras can help in this. The word "chakra" comes from the Sanskrit (from India) and means "wheel". The chakras connect your etheric bodies with your physical body. They are your personal energy centers, where the main themes of your life are recorded.

Your invisible bodies are only visible to clairvoyant/clairaudient people and detectible for those with extra-sensory perception. All indigenous peoples of the earth transmit the knowledge of the energy centers from generation to generation. In the west, the eastern chakra teachings are especially widespread. These teach of the seven main chakras. The "Chakra Tree of Life" refers to these chakras. These areas in the tree correspond to the main themes of the individual chakras.

In assessing your tree according to the wisdom of the "Tree of Life", the highest and lowest parts as well as the heart-region should be given the most attention. Additionally, it is important how much of the paper your tree fills up, i.e., that all areas are full of life.

The following points will help you assess your drawing:
- If the roots of your tree fill the page, each of your chakras is developed. You are a holistic personality, "at home" on every plane. One exception, however, is the assistance tree, which is quite small and placed in the center of the page. These individuals also have holistic potential, but in a small, defined sphere.
- Does your tree have a wide-spread crown? This indicates that you are full of ideas. You are a visionary personality.
- A clear boundary to the crown indicates personal blockages. This individual is not living out their full potential. This blockage can also come from drugs or other medications.

Another possibility is deep fear and uncertainty. Some people hide behind a mask. This clear demarcation is often present in highly-sensitive people, who are clairvoyant, clairaudient, or empathic. These people are often not even aware that they have extra-sensory abilities. They are afraid to exercise these gifts.
- Missing roots indicate a lack of stability and sense of basic trust. These people struggle with self-confidence and self-awareness, or have recurrent problems with these themes. They also lack grounding, i.e., contact with Mother Earth, and have a tendency to live with their head in the clouds. They struggle with reality and sometimes have the feeling of being in the wrong place.
- If there are no leaves in the heart area (transition from trunk to crown), protection is lacking and the person can be very sensitive.

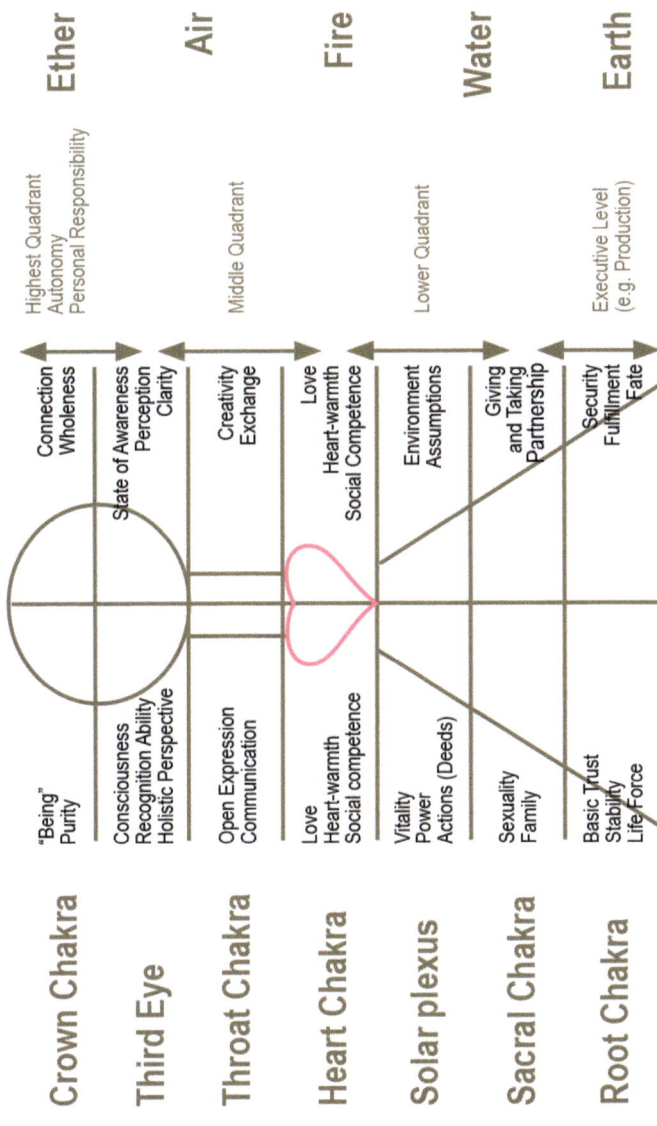

Use the "Chakra Tree of Life" together with the questions to assess your tree. Answer the questions in relation to your personality. Take the areas (chakras) that are missing especially into consideration. Missing, undeveloped areas are areas that your tree does not adequately cover, given its size. Some people's trees do not extend down to the bottom of the paper. Depending on how high you drew your tree, the bottom areas (such as root or sacral chakra) and their themes could be lacking in your life. Conversely, some people's trees don't extend to the top of the page. These people are lacking in the higher areas, such as third eye or crown chakra. If your tree does not extend into some areas, this means that those are areas you still need to develop.

Remember that the tree drawing is an intuitive test. Trust your first impulse as you assess it. Use the classical tree analysis and the "Chakra Tree of Life" to assess yourself, personally. What can you learn from this exercise? What does it tell you about yourself?

Tips and Tricks

The "Chakra Tree of Life" is an excellent way to demonstrate a person's potential. Moreover, blockages and personal issues are clearly visible in the drawing. The self-test can give a first impression of your personality. However, it is worthwhile to consult an expert for an in-depth analysis. In addition to the assessment, an expert can assist the client to release the existing issues. An analysis is an interesting way to learn more about yourself. But what really helps you evolve is concentrated work with another person and the release from debilitating and obstructive themes.

For independent work on yourself, there are a number of additional books and exercises available. Further options follow below.

Because the "Chakra Tree of Life" analysis is rather complex, there are an infinite number of tips and tricks. The possibilities are almost as large as there are people; because each person needs a different tool to advance on his path. To list all the variations would exceed the scope of this book. Below, you will find a selected list of helpful exercises and suggestions. I have emphasized options that are relatively easy and geared toward the people of today. The young, sensitive generation (indigo children, crystal children, Buddha personalities, New Age Children) will benefit from this collection.

EXERCISE: Release difficult and old themes

If your tree is placed more in the past (left side of the paper) than in the future (right side), you should complete the following exercise. Think about what is still weighing on your mind and standing in your way. Let go of your heavy past by imaging it as a stone. Connect each issue with one stone. If you do not know what is bothering you right now, then say: "I charge all these stones with the issues that I want to release at this time." Imagine the burden and the issues flowing into the stones. Then imagine tossing them back over your shoulder. Notice how this feels. Did you feel how a weight left you? You can also perform this exercise physically with real stones.

The exercise works even if you do not feel anything. The effect unfolds in your sub-consciousness. It is important that you believe in the effectiveness of the exercise, because thoughts have power. Your thoughts can become reality and their effects will become known.

Open Crowns

People who draw an open crown on their tree are visionary and imaginative. They are constantly consciously (or unconsciously) in connection with the etheric world. Depending on how these people have developed their potential, they may have contact with spirit beings or may be connected with the invisible matrix (e.g., Akashic records). This invisible matrix has recorded all the knowledge of this earth. It carries all of mankind's thoughts in it. This channel to 'heaven' is permanently open (open tree crown) in many great scientists, artists, as well as people in clinics for the mentally ill. That is why these people are sometimes no longer present with themselves, they snap, or become ill in other ways. Usually, these people are quite normal. They just need to learn how to deal with their sensitive gifts. This channel can remain permanently open, because it provides nourishment for the nervous system and is a source of inspiration. Light should always flow into it. It is good for our nerves and nourishment for our physical body. Light carries all the nutrients and vital substances that a person needs.

Sensitive People

A glance at a person's face and at their tree can be enough to see if they have extra-sensory abilities. Clairvoyant people often have one or two notches between their eyebrows. These are lines in the skin that look almost like incisions.

There are many businessmen and women who are not aware of their abilities. Many of them use their sensitive potential for their ideas in everyday business. They are visionary and gifted. They get their ideas through images, an inner voice, or through feelings. These images, voices, and feelings are the language of their intuition. How does your inspiration speak to you? Think about how you receive ideas. Do they come through images, an inner voice? Or is it a feeling? Multiple channels can be simultaneously active, of course.

What matters is that you recognize what is within you. It is your immeasurable potential. Those who recognize their potential can perceive and fulfill their mission in life; and whoever lives their potential has a sense of trust and well-being. This person lives as who and what he is. He is a tower of strength that cannot be easily disturbed. He experiences a sense of fulfillment.

Missing Roots

People who have not drawn any roots would benefit from the tree meditation. It is very important that they mentally anchor themselves, so that they remain in the here and now. Otherwise, they will tend to float off to other dimensions when their daily life is not going as they would like. They lose sight of reality, have trouble with their lives, and are therefore more vulnerable.

EXERCISE: Dropping an Anchor

You can do this exercise with your eyes open or shut. It is short, effective, and only takes a few seconds.

Imagine an anchor. This represents all your energy bodies (physical, emotional, Inner Fire, mental, and spiritual bodies). Take care how your anchor hangs; it is important that it is perfectly straight, with the tip pointing down. If it is tilted or inverted, straighten it. Anchor it deep in Mother Earth. Sense how this anchoring feels. Be aware of this "completeness" and alignment and spread this feeling through your physical body with gratitude.

In case you cannot imagine an anchor, complete the exercise in your thoughts and with your intuition. Trust your inner voice and your feelings. Off-center or inverted anchors indicate that a person is not entirely in their physical body. This person does not feel good in their skin or is helter-skelter. Clairvoyant people see this "off-centeredness" of the energetic bodies. The displacement can be caused by shocks of negative experiences. There are people who have not been truly present in their physical bodies for years and do not realize it. For them, this state has become normal.

Open Heart Region

If the transition from the stem to the crown of the tree is drawn without leaves, this indicates a very sensitive and vulnerable person. These people need to learn to recognize their boundaries and to communicate them clearly to other people. Say "no" when you want to say "no" and "yes" to things that you really want. An honest "no" is worth more than doing something that you don't want to. Over 90% of people will unconsciously know if you really mean it or not. You can only lie to 10% of a person's perceptions with your words and acts. Take care that you define your boundaries with love. It is important that you are completely clear with yourself about what you want. Clearness sends out clear energy. Sometimes those around you will only realize that you said or did the right thing after-the-fact. You cannot please everyone. Be your own best friend first. This is self-love. When you do this, you will feel good and you will have a lot of energy, which will also benefit those around you.

Assistance Trees

The typical assistance tree is small and placed in the center of the sheet. Assistance personalities need a small and defined place in which to completely develop. Assistance personalities need to become aware of their entire potential. It is important that they realize that they need a small, manageable job or sphere of influence. They can fully contribute and experience their potential in this domain. They are ideal assistants or could work in management in a big company, where their responsibilities and duties are clearly defined and straightforward.

Develop Missing Areas

With the chakra Tree of Life analysis, you can discover what you still need to develop. With the help of meditations for the affected chakra(s) or with a chakra handbook, you can continue to work on the appropriate themes (see Bibliography). Good chakra books have exercises to balance your chakras. My book "The Key to Happiness" also supports you in developing your chakras and your full potential.

Through energetic work with hands or crystals, which you can lay on the corresponding chakra, you can also balance your energy. This dissolves blockages and the respective problems are set in motion. Now you have the opportunity to consciously work on and live out these themes in your daily life. Practice self-awareness by adopting a confident manner in meetings or exchanges with others. Make sure that your feet are firmly planted on the ground and that your legs are hip-wide. Be consciously aware of the power of Mother Earth and draw on this energy for what you say and do.

EXERCISE: Chakra Balancing

1. Using the "Chakra Tree of Life, determine which chakras need to be balanced. Trust your intuition for this analysis.
2. Make yourself comfortable and consciously breathe into the corresponding chakra. You can perform this exercise lying down, sitting, or standing. As you exhale, release. Let everything that is weighing you, is difficult, or is blocking you flow back to whence it came.
3. Use your hands to support you. Lay them over the corresponding energy center. You will find the location of each chakra in the section: Chakra – Energy Levels. Take deep, conscious breaths. As you inhale, stretch open the funnel of your energy center that emanates from your physical body. As you exhale, draw the energy back in. Let your breath flow and repeat this exercise until you feel relaxed.
4. If you are still not feeling better and the energy is not flowing uniformly through your chakras, use your hands. Trust your intuition as you assess the flow of energy. This wisdom is innate in you. Circle your hand counter-clockwise over the chakra, to create a spiral from the inside out. This movement releases blockages.
5. Smooth out the blockages that are ready to be released. Imagine you are holding them in your hand and, in one gesture, draw them out of your body and throw them away. Of course, this exercise also works on an energetic level.
6. If you sense that the heaviness has left, trace a clockwise circle on your chakra with your hand.
7. Conclude this exercise my resting both hands on your energy center again. Take a few deep and deliberate breaths.
8. Dedicate yourself once again to your everyday life and trust the power of this exercise.

To Do

This is a list of concrete steps that will help you reach your goal and develop your potential. Considering your tree, think about specific things you can do to further develop yourself. The previously mentioned 'Tips and Tricks' will help you.

Questions for you to consider:
1. What does my tree want to tell me?
2. Is there anything that especially impresses me?
3. Where does my potential lie?
4. What is my as-of-yet untapped potential?
5. How can I develop it?
6. What steps do I need to take immediately and which steps can I introduce gradually?
7. Am I going to go through this process alone, or do I want support?

You will find suggestions of steps to take in order to develop your potential in respect to harmonizing your chakras in the section: Chakra – Recognize your Energy Levels.

Personal Insights

At the end of this exercise or before you go to bed, take a moment and answer the following questions spontaneously:
- What personal insights did I gain from this exercise?
- What points will I follow in the future?
- When will I begin to apply these insights?

Putting things in writing creates commitment. What has proven to work in business, is also worthwhile for your personal intentions and projects. Write down your insights and "to-dos". Generate small, realistic steps that you are sure to accomplish.

Inner Team – Identify your Personality Type

The foundation of the personality typology is based on the archetypes of C.G. Jung. This model includes the four basic psychological functions: thinking, feeling, sensing, and intuition. A person's personality includes all four areas as well as the Inner Fire, the heart consciousness of man. These basic functions are also referred to as a person's "Inner Team".

Self-test: Inner Team

Complete the self-test when you have a quiet moment. The main focus of this test is an assessment of your "Inner Team". Award each team member 1-5 points. For example, the Thinker might receive 5 points if those characteristics are especially strong. If emotions are not your strong suite, the Feeler would receive 1 point.

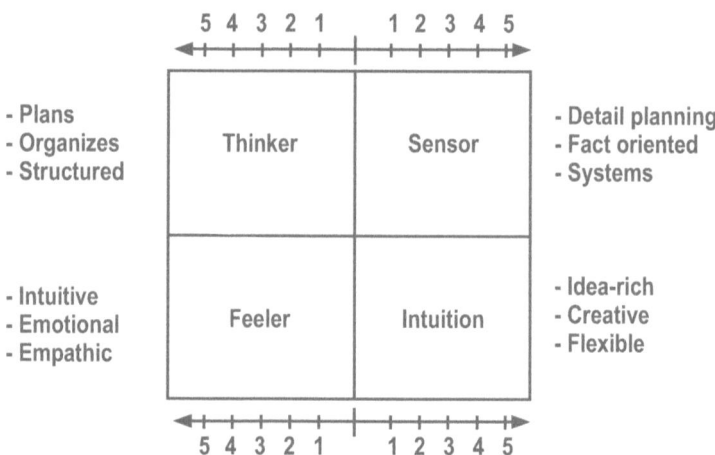

Assess your "Inner Team" spontaneously. Ask yourself how strongly you experience and use each area.

External Test: Personality Typology

The external test can be completed alone or by someone that you know. If you complete this part of the exercise yourself, try to see yourself from the perspective of someone close to you and ask yourself how they would assess your "Inner Team".

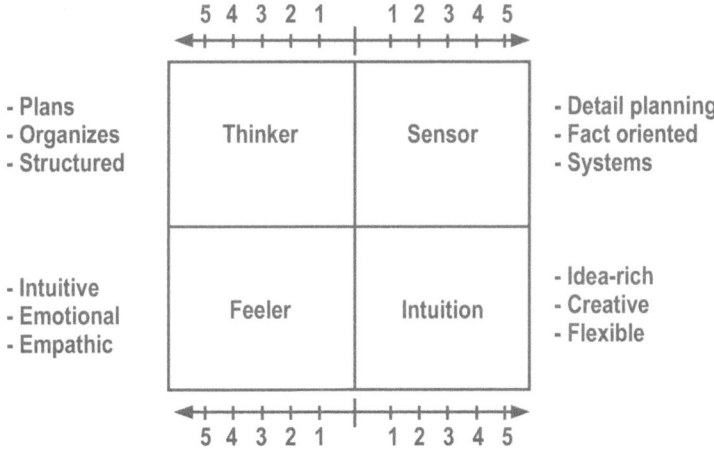

Average: "Inner Team"

Average the values from the self and external tests. The result is your personality typology. This assessment shows how balanced and whole you are. You can then see where you can continue to work to develop your potential.

The team members who received less than 3 points indicate areas that still need to grow. These levels have been less developed. Your untapped potential lies there.

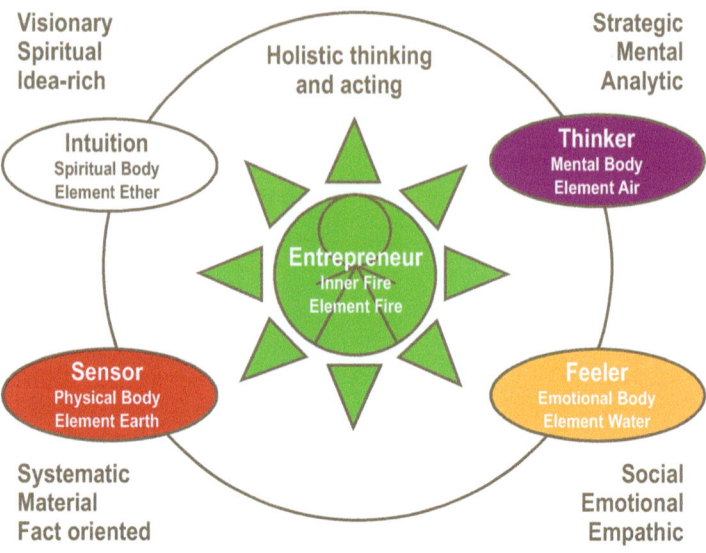

The Inner Team

The personality typology provides information as to how an individual's "Inner Team" of Intuitive, Thinker, Perceiver, Sensor, and Entrepreneur/Inner Fire are put together. It shows which personality aspects dominate and which have been neglected. The individual team composition also provides information about a person's competencies and abilities. Once you know what they are, you can use them selectively in your professional and personal life and draw on their powers. Ideally, each person should be able to rely on the competencies and abilities of their "Inner Team" according to the situation they find themselves in. Here are the members of your Inner Team:

- **The Perceiver (Body):** This team member processes everything that you receive through the five senses. It corresponds to a person's material body of a person with all its organs, cells, and constitution.
- **The Sensor (Emotions):** This team member is concerned with people and how they are doing and how they feel. The Sensor has the ability to sense what others are feeling and to understand their actions and behavior. This is the socially competent team member. It senses, saves, and processes emotions.
- **The Thinker (Mind):** This team member is the rational side of a person. It is the thinker, planner, analyst, and organizer. It is the "heady" side of your team. This level holds specialized knowledge and saves thoughts, principles and doctrines.
- **The Intuitive (Spirit):** This team member is responsible for creative insights and innovative ideas. These insights are often referred to as "gut feelings". Philosophers and inventors such as Plato and Albert Einstein were experienced on this level and drew their knowledge and wisdom from this team member. Intuition draws its information from the sub-conscious, which, according to brain science research,

comprises about 90% of brain function. These insights come in the form of sudden inspiration, images, or feelings. Because these insights are not rationally comprehensible, many people do not trust their intuition.

- **The Entrepreneur (Inner Fire)** Entrepreneur personalities are ideal teachers, healers, and coaches. Their "Inner Team" is balanced, which means that each team member received 3 or more points. They are holistic personalities, who feel at home at every level. Entrepreneurs can complete a project from beginning to end entirely by themselves. They have access to all the abilities and competencies of their "Inner Team" and actively engage them. They live from their center and have a lot of fire. That is why I call this area the "Inner Fire".

Consider the composition of your "Inner Team". When you look at your team's distribution, what does that mean for you? Look especially at the team members who received less than 3 points. You have the possibility to develop these areas. Think about what benefits you would gain from developing them. One gain could be an increase in your long-term well-being and overall performance.

Put yourself in the shoes of your Sensor, for example. Suppose that you have been paying too little attention to this team member and have not been taking care of her needs. How would she react? She would probably be unhappy, sick, and would really like to quit her job with you! Her bad attitude is going to pass on to the other team members at some point, so that the overall team feeling is gray. Not a very good working atmosphere! Your performance and satisfaction will slowly and consistently decrease. Balance is important for a happy and fulfilled life.

Tips and Tricks

Every person carries all abilities within them and can further develop them. You only have to want it. Look at babies. They come whole to this world and are shaped over time according to their conditioning. The more a person is allowed to be themselves, from the first step on, the more likely it is that he will be able to express its inborn abilities and full potential as an adult. Some very strong personalities are able to grow and remain true to themselves in the face of challenges and external influences. In today's wave of change, there are more and more people who jump on that wave of transformation and swim with it. These people find their way back to their true nature. They find their way to wholeness and unity.

There will always be people who are able to change more easily and those who really struggle with it. The degree of consciousness plays a very important role in process of change and development. Where there's a will, there's a way. For example, managers and directors with less-developed empathy can increase their social competency with colleagues, clients, and other people.

Physical Pain

Physical pain like headaches, fevers, and back/neck pain can actually have its source at the spiritual, mental, or emotional level. This pain is the body's SOS, an indication that you should stop, slow down, and take some time out for yourself. It is worthwhile to give your attention to all your body's levels and to react to early warning signs. You should especially pay attention to areas with less than 3 points.

Leadership Qualities

A person's leadership abilities can be seen through their professional, social, and conceptual qualities. These three components can be linked to an executive's "Inner Team":

- The professional abilities correspond to the Thinker and Perceiver.
- The social abilities belong to the Sensor.
- The conceptual abilities come from the Intuitive.

Using this link, the leadership qualities of a particular executive can be seen from the individual composition of his team. The "Inner Team" also shows a person's untapped potential. The "Inner Team" is the key to personal and professional success.

For a project to be successful, it is crucial how the "Inner Team" is being used. In professional projects, it makes sense to distribute the tasks according to the skills and competencies of each team member. In a company, the controller is not expected to do the job of the human resource manager and the developer is not responsible for production. The same is true for the "Inner Team". Ideally, the team would be deployed as follows, taking into consideration the team member's skills: The Intuitive would bring the ideas and develop the vision; the Thinker would be responsible for planning and organization; the Perceiver would look after the general well-being and motivation throughout the project (the leadership thoughts); and the Sensor would be responsible for the implementation and detailed planning.

A successful executive (and self-management is also an executive position), has professional, social, and conceptual competencies to smaller or greater degrees depending on the field of work. An executive must always have strong social competence, which means he must know how to deal with other people. His level of specific trade knowledge is high at the lower levels of management, and decreases as you rise through management levels; it is exactly the opposite for conceptual ability. The king of executives, however, is the "Entrepreneur". This is a personality who thinks and acts entrepreneurially, i.e., he has a high level of professional, social, and conceptual skills. Entrepreneurs can complete a project from beginning to end entirely by themselves and step in to fill gaps in the company. If there are a lot of people in a company who are technically strong, but who do not interact well personally or who cannot see the company as a whole, this points to a social and conceptual deficit.

Recently, a study attempted to answer the question: What percentage of executives are "entrepreneurs". Personality profiles of 400 executives and students were analyzed at a University in Switzerland. The main query of the study was the distribution of the "Inner Team" (i.e., the Thinker, the Perceiver, the Feeler, and the Intuitive) of each test subject. The results of the personality profiles gave the following picture: Only about a third of executives are "entrepreneurs".

To Do

To dos are specific steps that help you reach your goals. Think about what your "Inner Team" should look like and develop concrete actions to reach your goal. Team members with less than 3 points indicate untapped potential. Of course, you can also set a goal for yourself to further train or use the rest of the aspects. Do you want, for example, to further develop your Sensor? Then look at the description of the Sensor and ask yourself which skills you still need to develop. You can train empathy, for example, by imagining yourself in someone else's skin. Put yourself in their situation and life. How do you feel? Can you better understand that person's behavior?

Questions to think about:
1. How can I develop my untapped potential (areas with less than 3 points)?
2. To which areas do I pay too little attention in my professional and personal lives?
3. Do I listen to every team members' opinion?
4. Do I use each team member according to their abilities?
5. Which of my team members does not feel good? How can I improve this situation?

Possible actions to develop your "Inner Team":
- **Intuitive**
  Painting, crafting, brainstorming, meditation
- **Thinker**
  Continuing education, reading, implementing time management, developing strategies

- **Sensor**
  Practice empathy with others, i.e., imagine yourself in someone else's shoes, play with children, and try to see things from a child's perspective
- **Perceiver**
  Write down your thoughts, engage in physical activity (e.g., jogging), detail planning (i.e., think through and write down every step of a project down to the smallest detail)

Personal Insights

At the end of this exercise or before you go to bed, take a moment and answer the following questions spontaneously:
- What personal insights do I take from this exercise?
- What points will I follow in the future?
- When will I begin to apply these insights?

Tree Meditation: Connecting Above and Below

Disconnect, release, and recharge. Treat yourself to a moment of peace in a time of change and development. Leave your troubles behind. Immerse yourself in a calm and relaxed atmosphere. Discover your personal strengths through the tree meditation. Strengthen your self-awareness, your self-confidence, your self-assurance, and your stability. Consciously appreciate your potential and develop it.

Procedure:
1. Assume a comfortable position, sitting or lying down. Turn off all sources of disturbance, e.g., cell phones, telephones, etc., so that you won't be interrupted.
2. Close your eyes; inhale and exhale deeply through your nose. Place both hands on your bellybutton. Feel how your belly rises as you inhale and sinks as you exhale. Follow the breath-flow with your thoughts. If other thoughts come up, let them pass through like clouds across the sky. Thoughts come and go. Let them go.
3. Imagine you are inhaling new strength and motivation with every inhale and with every exhale, releasing everything old, heavy, and burdensome. Leave your everyday behind you with every exhale. With every release, you become more calm and relaxed. You become more and more deeply relaxed.
4. Imagine you are a tree. Your trunk is from your feet up to your chest. The treetop is from your chest upwards to the highest point of your head, at the crown.
5. Roots grow from the soles of your feet down to the middle of Mother Earth. They are big, strong roots. Let the roots grow out from the soles of your feet. Fill up on the strength of Mother Earth through these roots. Draw this energy up through the soles of your feet into your physical body. Nourish every cell, every pore, and every part of your physical body with this strength. Paint yourself interior with the light of Moth-

er Earth. Draw it up through your legs into your upper body and let it stream out through your shoulders into your hands. Draw this light into your head and let it flow out through your crown chakra, the highest point of your head. Paint your aura, the invisible sphere that surrounds your physical body with this light. This sphere is your charisma, your 'vibe', and shows your amazing potential. Fill it up completely with the strength of Mother Earth.

6. Now, connect with the sun above your head. Absorb the yellow-gold light of the sun through your leaves. Draw this power into your physical body. Nourish every cell, every pore, and every part of your physical body with the power of the sun. Paint yourself within with this gold-yellow light. Let it stream down through your physical body and flow out through the soles of your feet. Finally, nourish your aura with this sunlight as well. Mix the colors of the sun with the light of Mother Earth.

7. Observe your aura, the personal space surrounding you. Is it as big as it should be? If not, extend your aura as far as it should go. Rest for a moment in this expansion.

8. Take a few more deep breaths. Re-affirm the power of the tree meditation. Spread this power throughout your physical body.

9. When you are ready, open your eyes. Return consciously to your daily life.

WHERE AM I NOW?

In this part of the book, you will receive answers to the following questions: What personality type am I? Who Am I? Who should I be? What is my path? What do I need at the present time? What should I pay attention to on my journey?

The path that you will take through the individual tests and meditations will help you to find your personal balance. You will recognize which specific steps will bring you further on your way. What is important is your personal initiative. It's up to you, to incorporate them into your daily life. Success lies in your hand.

Colors – Become Aware of Your Personal Attributes

Even Goethe was interested in colors and their meanings. His color theory is his most comprehensive work. He saw it as the basis of his existence. In the last century, Swiss Professor Lüscher also explored the effect of colors on the human psyche.

Self-Test

In this self-test, colors are used to obtain information about your own personality. The following questions are the focus of the analysis:
- What characteristics are attributed to my personality (P is)?
- What should my personality be like (P should be)?
- How can I develop my personality (path)?

You can choose from the following colors:
- Blue
- Yellow
- Green
- Bright green
- Orange
- Red
- Violet
- White
- Pink
- Light pink
- Silver
- Gold
- Brown

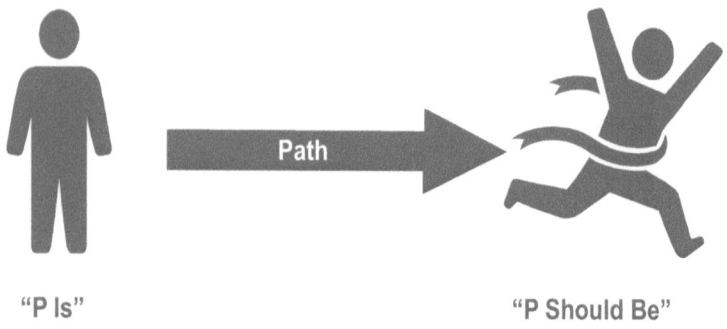

"P Is"   "P Should Be"

Spontaneously pick one color from this list for each of the following themes:
1. My personality as it is now ("P is").
2. The way ("path") that lies before me and which will lead me from "P is" to "P should be".
3. My personality as it should be ("P should be").

Write down the colors for "P is", "P should be", and "path" that first speak to you. Only read the meaning of the colors at the end of the exercise; otherwise, your results could be distorted.

Color Meanings

Every color is assigned specific qualities and effects that can be applied in reference to your own personality. The color significance is independent of culture, language, or race and is the same for all humans. Even people who are color blind can complete this exercise.

The colors have the following meanings:
- **Blue**
Confidence, depth, coolness, calm, distance, aloofness, introversion
- **Brown**
Stability, reality
- **Yellow**
Vitality, happiness, flexibility, joie de vivre, communication
- **Gold**
Clear thinking, deep joy, seeing the whole
- **Green**
Hope, harmony, feeling side of life, health, compassion, well-being, contentment
- **Bright Green**
Healing abilities, healing
- **Orange**
Joie de vivre, insight, wisdom, perceiving through emotion
- **Pink**
Pure, unconditional love (Christ consciousness)
- **Light pink**
Friendliness, gentleness, love, harmony
- **Red**
Power, leadership spirit, motivation, courage, spirit of development, extroversion
- **Silver**
Knowledge, purity
- **Violet**
Transformation, development, spiritual perfection, healing
- **White**
Purity, clarity, wisdom, serenity, resolution

Once you have selected the three colors, read through the color meanings and put them in relation to your personality. Suppose you are in a professional transition and you have selected yellow for "P should be". Ask yourself what the symbolism of this color could mean for you personally and specifically for your transition. Yellow shows, for example, that joy and vitality are important. This means that your new job should promote and encourage these wishes. So ask yourself what job would bring you joy. From this point on, only apply for jobs at companies that really speak to you. When you go for an interview, make sure that you get a chance to speak with the team that you'll be working with. Because everything that surrounds you influences you, consciously and unconsciously.

Tips and Tricks

Colors affect our bodies, our emotions, our understanding, and our spirits. That is why colors can be used to deliberately support our processes of change and development. Green, blue, purple, and white are relaxing; red, orange, and yellow are energizing. A person low on energy, burnt out, or sad should surround themselves with energizing colors. You could, for example, hang pictures with these colors on your walls or choose your clothes, underclothes, or tie accordingly. Mental exercises using colors can have the same effect.

Brain research has shown that the human brain cannot distinguish between reality and imagination. An idea, a visualization of an inner image if, for the brain, already the reality.

EXERCISE: Color-Balance

After the color test, the color-balance exercise provides an opportunity to go a little deeper. It is a subtle exercise that affects the unconscious levels. The effect depends on the color.

Procedure:
1. Assume a position in which you easily relax. Turn off your cell phone and other sources of disturbance if possible and close your eyes. Inhale and exhale deeply through your nose. Your abdomen rises with the inhale and lowers with the exhale. Take deep, even breaths. Leave your worries behind you by exhaling two or three times through your mouth. Focus your concentration inwards during the entire exercise by following the flow of your breath. If other thoughts arise, imagine they are clouds. Let them pass by.
2. With every inhalation, imagine that you are drawing in new strength and inspiration; with every exhalation, imagine that you are releasing everything heavy that is blocking you. Repeat this breathing exercise until you are totally relaxed.
3. Continue with the exercise. Imagine the three colors of the "P is", "path", and "P should be" lying before you on the floor. Imagine you are standing on the "is" and allow that color to flow up through your feet and into your entire body. Stain every cell, every part of your physical body with this color. In your imagination, travel through your body and guide the color into the tips of your fingers and toes and up into your head. When you have finished, imagine the color pouring out of your crown chakra at the highest point of your head like a fountain and surrounding your entire body. Repeat this process with the color you chose for your "path" and end with your "P should be" color.
4. Open your eyes and consciously return to your surroundings.
5. Allow yourself to be surprised by the effects of this exercise.

EXERCISE: Cleansing Meditation

As the name already says, this meditation cleanses.

Procedure:
1. Assume a comfortable position sitting or lying down. Turn off all sources of interruption (e.g., cell phone, telephone) so that you will not be disturbed.
2. Close your eyes and inhale and exhale deeply through your nose. Rest both hands on your belly button. Feel how your abdomen rises with the inhale and falls with the exhale. Follow your breath flow with your thoughts. If other thoughts appear, let them pass by you like clouds. Thoughts come and go. Let them go.
3. Image you are standing under a waterfall. The water is clear blue and completely clean. Let the water fall down over your shoulders. Feel the water on your shoulders, imagine that it is washing away all blockages and burdens from you. The water is the exact temperature that you prefer.
4. The water is now streaming to your crown chakra, inside your head, and through your entire body. Imagine the water flowing through your head, over your shoulders, in your arms, and down to your fingertips. It flows through your upper body down into your hips, your thighs, calves, and to the tips of your toes. Open the soles of your feet and let the water flow out through your body into the earth. Let the water flow in through your head and out through your feet a few times. Follow the water as it flows out of your body. Remain in this exercise as long as you want to and until you feel fresh and motivated again. You can always add on another exercise. You can also simply dwell in the "being", in the calm/stillness. In this state of being, your attention is completely focused within and your rational brain is turned completely off. Wait, without expectations, for what comes. Maybe you will see colors, images, or feel a pleasant feeling.
5. End the meditation by opening your eyes and focusing on your body and your surroundings. If you feel like it, stretch a bit, and move your arms and legs.

EXERCISE: Transformation Meditation

- Assume a comfortable position sitting or lying down. Turn off all sources of interruption (e.g., cell phone, telephone) so that you will not be disturbed.
- Close your eyes and inhale and exhale deeply through your nose. Rest both hands on your belly button. Feel how your abdomen rises with the inhale and falls with the exhale. Follow your breath flow with your thoughts. If other thoughts appear, let them pass by you like clouds. Thoughts come and go. Let them go.
- As you inhale, imagine violet light is streaming in through your crown chakra, the top-most point of your head, into your physical body. Let this color stream into every pore, every cell, every part or your physical body. See your body with your inner eye. Let the violet color flow into the dark parts and corners. Violet transforms. It releases anything negative and burdensome. Trust what you feel in your body. Let the color flow wherever you sense that you need it. Maybe your inner voice gives you an image or an impulse. Trust your intuition. Stay present in those blocked places until they have released. At the end of the meditation, every part of your physical body should be filled with violet light.
- Now, let the violet stream from above pass down through your body. It connects you with heaven and earth.
- The violet stream grows into a great pillar of light around you. This is your personal space, which gives you stability and support. The light pillar helps you stay present in your light during times of upheaval. You can complete your processes without being disturbed or influenced from without. Be aware of the power of the violet light.
- Return to your personal middle, to your heart chakra in the middle of your chest. Enclose the power of this meditation in this space and carry it with you into your daily life. Whenever you consciously focus on your heart chakra, you will call up the effect of this meditation.
- Open your eyes when you feel ready. Return with awareness to your daily life and trust the effects of the transformation meditation.

EXERCISE: Stress Reduction

The position of the forehead and the back of the head can reduce stress and bring a clear head. This position can also be used for target programming or to release a stressful experience.

Procedure:
- Assume a comfortable position sitting or lying down. Turn off all sources of interruption (e.g., cell phone, telephone) so that you will not be disturbed.
- You can complete this exercise with your eyes open or closed. Inhale and exhale deeply through your nose, lightly holding your forehead and the back of your head. It is also very comfortable when another person holds your head.

EXERCISE: Thymus Tapping

Tapping the thymus energizes. It can be used, for example, before tests or talks, against tiredness, or when fighting a cold.

Procedure: Tap rhythmically a few times on your thymus. It is located approximately one hand's width below the pit of your throat.

EXERCISE: Wayne Cook (Centering Exercise)

This exercise balances, centers, and brings inner peace.

Procedure:
Perform this exercise for both sides of your body. Remove your shoes and sit down. Cross one leg over the other and grasp your toes with your hand. Hold your hand so that your fingertips are touching the arch of your foot, if possible. With your other hand, hold your ankle. Remain a moment in this position. When you are done, place both feet hip-wide flat on the floor. Bring your hands slowly together in front of you until your fingertips touch. Repeat with the other side.

EXERCISE: Three Thumps (Revitalizing Exercise)

This exercise balances your body and increases concentration. It also strengthens, revitalizes, and relieves stress.

Procedure:
Tap a few times with both the second and third fingers on the points marked in the image below. Tap the kidney points, K-27, and the neuro-lymphatic points on both sides simultaneously.

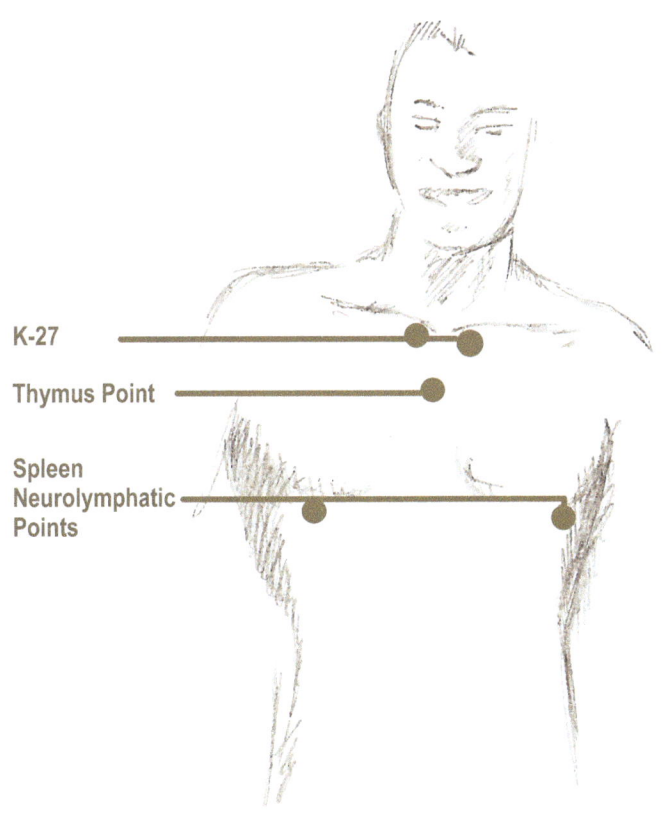

EXERCISE: Lemon Meditation

The yellow of the lemon together with its sour taste is refreshing. This meditation stimulates and motivates. It also promotes imagination.

Procedure:
- Assume a comfortable position sitting or lying down. Turn off all sources of interruption (e.g., cell phone, telephone) so that you will not be disturbed.
- Close your eyes and inhale and exhale deeply through your nose. Rest both hands on your belly button. Feel how your abdomen rises with the inhale and falls with the exhale. Follow your breath flow with your thoughts. If other thoughts appear, let them pass by you like clouds. Thoughts come and go. Let them go.
- Imagine you are holding a lemon in your hand. Observe it. Feel the lemon peel in your hand. Imagine you take a knife and cut a piece out. Bite in this piece and feel the sour taste in your mouth. Let the juice run through your entire body. You can intensify this meditation by giving the juice a yellow hue.
- End the meditation by opening your eyes and focusing on your body and environment.

EXERCISE: Mirror Technique

The mirror technique is a method that promotes an understanding of oneself and others and that reveals our blind spots. These are personal aspects that we do not want to see in ourselves. For this exercise, others are seen as mirrors of our own personality. One example is the statement: "Every boss gets the employees he deserves".

Procedure:
1. Think of a person or situation that recently annoyed you. Or think about someone's behavior that bothers you.
2. Write down this behavior. What bothers you precisely?
3. Then ask yourself how this behavior reflects you. Or what you should learn from this situation.
4. Write these insights on the paper as well.
5. If you cannot see anything reflected to you in this behavior, you should seek feedback from a trusted friend or qualified counselor.

EXERCISE: Color Breath

Do this exercise with a color of your choice. The effect varied depending on the color, stretching from invigorating to calming: If you want to relax, take blue; red is activating and grounding; yellow motivates and revitalizes.

Procedure:
- For this exercise, choose the first color you spontaneously see. Trust your first impulse; this is your intuition. It is telling you which color is good for you. Take the test by reading the meaning of the selected color. You will see what is applicable to your situation.
- Assume a comfortable position sitting or lying down. Turn off all sources of interruption (e.g., cell phone, telephone) so that you will not be disturbed.
- Close your eyes and inhale and exhale deeply through your nose. Rest both hands on your belly button. Feel how your abdomen rises with the inhale and falls with the exhale. Follow your breath flow with your thoughts. If other thoughts appear, let them pass by you like clouds. Thoughts come and go. Let them go.
- Continue with the exercise when you have relaxed a bit. Imagine you are inhaling your chosen color through your nose.

As you exhale, let this color flow through your entire physical body. Stain every cell, every pore, and every part of your body this particular color. Travel through your body with your thoughts and draw the color into the tips of your fingers and toes.
- After some time, let the color stream out of your body so that it stretches into a kind of sphere or egg around you and completely encloses you. Choose a geometric form that speaks to you. The idea that you are sitting in an egg or sphere is a mental exercise that helps you stay present with yourself. Therapists, who want to protect themselves from their client's moods, visualize a sphere around themselves and around their clients, for example. Blue and violet are strong protective colors. This exercise is also useful for managers who are prepping for a difficult meeting, for example. It helps you maintain a certain distance from the situation.

To Do

Read again the meanings of the colors that you selected. Pay special attention to the color that you chose for your "path". This color will show you which themes are most present in your current personal development. Write down specific actions to take for the most important points when you are done. For example, for someone who has chosen white as their "path" color, it can be important to release the old and to find clarity about the journey before them. For someone who has chosen green for their "path" color, they should pay more attention to their health and well-being.

Questions for personal reflection:
- What themes are my color selections highlighting for me?
- What do these themes mean to me, personally?
- How can I apply these themes in my daily life?
- Which specific actions will support me in their application?
- Which actions have the highest priority?

- Which actions should I complete today?
- What factors are hindering me in their application? How can I alleviate them?
- Who could help me in this?

Possible actions to progress along your path and to develop yourself further:

- **Pink**

  The color of unconditional love lets your heart speak and allows you to listen to your heart. Take this sentence to heart: It is only with the heart that one can see rightly. But unconditional love does not mean that you have to put up with everything. You should respect your boundaries and communicate them clearly.

- **Light Pink**

  Consciously let love flow into your life. Do something good for yourself. Accept yourself and others as you/they are. Respect your own and other's boundaries.

- **Gold**

  God's wisdom connects you with higher knowledge and allows you to communicate with the light-world, when you open yourself to it. Again and again, connect with the highest divine source: "God".

- **Silver**

  Silver is the color of the moon and feminine wisdom. Energize a glass of water at full or new moons. To do this, set a glass of water overnight by your window. You can mix this energy water (moon water) in a room spray or in your drink. A few drops are enough. Mix a few drops of essential oils, such as rose or lavender, to the room spray so that it smells good.

- **Brown**

  Connects you with Mother Nature. Take a walk in the woods or in the outdoors and consciously recharge. Establish contact with Mother Earth through conscious contact with the ground, by placing your feet firmly on the ground. You can also imagine that you are growing roots into the ground that stabilize you and bring you strength.

- **White**
  White carries the themes of purity and clarity. You gain purity by cleansing your body, your home, and your spheres of life. The cleansing meditation is perfect for this. It also works with energetic contamination, when you are carrying the energies and moods of other people inside of you. You obtain clarity when you allow yourself to take a break, for example, by going for a stroll in nature or practice one of the breathing exercises. You can also treat your soul to an energetic massage.
- **Violet**
  Transformation and development are needed. Think about which areas of your life or which personality traits you would like to change. Develop the appropriate measures to carry out these changes. Opportunities to develop yourself may include coaching, reading, conversations with trusted individuals, and seminars. Choose the option that most speaks to you and that you feel yourself spontaneously drawn to. In times of change, it is worthwhile it to give new options a chance. New brings growth. Violet is a color of transformation. Try the Transformation Meditation. Violet is also the color of the third eye. The seat of this chakra, which lies in the forehead, also corresponds to the intellectual level. People who live in their heads should turn off the thought-gears from time to time. The stress reduction exercise can be helpful here.
- **Blue**
  The color blue is associated with the throat chakra. It has to do with the themes: Communication and exchange. Gather the motivation you need before an interview with thymus tapping. Chimpanzees show us how to do it. Blue is also associated with the theme "calm and retreat". People who have chosen this color for their "path" should find ways to relax and meditate. Maybe you have another way to find peace?
- **Green**
  Green corresponds to health and your overall sense of well-being. Think about what you can do these days to support your health. Possible actions include getting enough to drink, con-

suming fresh fruits and vegetables, and making sure your diet is balanced and healthy. A relaxing bath in the evening after a full day of work, interesting conversations with those dear to you, and wearing comfortable clothing increases your sense of well-being. If you listen to your inner voice, you will certainly know what is good for you. Treat yourself to this gift today and in the coming days and weeks.

Green is also the color classically associated with the heart chakra. Your heart's desires are stored in this chakra. In the future, trust your heart more. It knows what is good for you and knows your deepest, hidden desires. Listen to the still, small voice and the subtle impulses that come from your personal center. You can strengthen your heart chakra with the Centering Exercise: Wayne Cook.

- **Light Green**
  This is the color of healing. Where do you need healing? Breathe deeply into this area and fill it with life energy with your breath. Accept the issues that it reveals to you with love. Allow yourself to feel them for a moment and then let them go. You are more than these things that weigh on you. Direct your thoughts daily to the Source of all Being (God). Consciously connect with this Source. Place yourself in this stream of light.
- **Yellow**
  Yellow is the color of joy and vitality. Think about the things that bring you joy. How can you increase your energy? Yellow is also the color of the solar plexus, your personal center of energy. This area is like a battery. The solar plexus is in the stomach area. Recharge this reservoir regularly, before your energy dissipates. Know and respect your personal boundaries. The Three Thumps exercise balances, regulates, and simultaneously energizes. The solar plexus is also connected with power issues. Do you exercise power over others? Or are you acting in love and for the benefit of all concerned? The Lemon Meditation is revitalizing and stimulating. Essential oils, such as lemon or lime, can be invigorating. These scents also improve concentration.

- **Orange**
  Orange is classically associated with the navel chakra. Themes such as partnership and your emotions are stored here. If you want to harmonize this area, surround yourself with the color orange. Buy orange towels for the bath, for instance. Essential oils such as orange or mandarin have a balancing effect. Another possibility to clarify relationships is the Mirror Technique. Orange is also a spiritual color. The Buddhist monks wear orange robes. So think about how you wish to experience spirituality in your daily life and how you want to make space for it in your life. It is on a spiritual, not a material level. It has to do with holistic thinking and the meaning of life. So ask yourself the following questions: Who am I? What can I do? Where am I headed and what does my path look like? What is my mission? You create a spiritual space in your life when you attend self-improvement classes with spiritual themes or read books on the subject. Be aware that a part of you is immaterial and therefore spiritual. Continue to allow all the planes of your being to express and develop themselves.
- **Red**
  Red is classically associated with the root chakra. Someone who is not grounded or rooted easily loses their footing. He is taken over by the emotions and moods of others and easily loses patience.
  Red indicates a spirit of leadership. Think about where you should take charge in your life and how you can express your leadership qualities. Who or what should you be guiding? Maybe it is time to look for a position with leadership responsibilities.

As you select your to-dos, keep in mind the themes associated with the color you chose for your "path". Also think about what actions you will implement immediately. Begin today, since they will be easily forgotten if you wait a few days. Build on the excitement and motivation of the moment.

Personal Insights

At the end of this exercise or before you go to bed, take a moment and answer the following questions spontaneously:
- What personal insights do I take from this exercise?
- What points will I follow in the future?
- When will I begin to apply these insights?

Cycles – Recognize Your Personal Rhythm

The seasons are nature's natural rhythm. People also have individual inner clocks and specific themes according to the phase of life. Original peoples still live according to nature and their inner clocks.

Self-Test: Cycles

Look at the images and choose the one that represents where you are now. Where are you personally and professionally?

Meaning of the Four Seasons

The seasons divide the year into different sections. They have different characteristics. The cycles/seasons can be correlated to your personal and professional standpoint. They show where you currently are.

The four seasons have the following significance:
- **Spring**
  New beginnings, awakening, development, change
- **Summer**
  Expansion, production, energy
- **Fall**
  Ripeness, harvest, enjoying what you have
- **Winter**
  Completion, retreat, regeneration, rest, peace, sleep

Tips and Tricks

Today's world picture points to alienation and denaturing. Some examples are the rapid change and growth of the economy, the high performance pressure, and the high labor turnover. On a personal level, the disasters manifest as anxiety, stress, burnout, and depression. One way to escape these tendencies is to take a step back to the natural cycles and phases of development. This means, taking a step back and returning to our personality. The more we can learn to follow our own personal rhythm and listen to our internal clock, the easier personal and professional decisions will be. Furthermore, we will feel happier and experience more balance; we can follow our life's path more easily and unburdened.

Spring

In spring, the birds sing more intensely than ever. They call their partners to couple. Nature awakens and begins to bloom until, just before summer, she appears in all her beauty.

Did you choose spring in your self-test? Then think about how you can integrate this season in your daily life. Where can you begin something new? Where you can express your creativity and develop your creative potential? Does your profession or your private environment allow for your awakening? Surely you can find ways to develop yourself. It may also be time to think about where it is necessary to bring about change. What can you, and what do you want to change? Listen to your heart, it will show you the way. Change takes time. Especially with family, each family member needs space to develop in their own way. In situations like this, it is also important to understand the other person and to trust that everything will turn out for the best. Listen to your inner impulses. Be clear about what you want and what makes sense for you in the long term.

	My one-year goals	My five-year goals
Personally		
Professionally		
Other		

EXERCISE: Plan for Future Success

Spring is a time of awakening and change. The next steps should be clear and precisely planned. Now is time to think about personal and professional goals.

Take a moment and think about what you want to achieve personally and professionally. Set specific goals. Where do you want to be in one year? In five years?

Career Coaching

Before you rush headlong into the next continuing education class, you should really be clear as to whether or not this new direction is really right for you. Maybe there are opportunities for further development at your current position, such as coaching.

Maybe only certain aspects are currently absent, such as the possibility to take on more responsibility, or to lead your own projects, but is the job as a whole the "right one"? Again, much can be achieved by careful positioning and coaching. Systematically developing your personal skills, such as learning team leadership or project planning, can help convince management to expand your responsibilities, thus ensuring greater satisfaction in both your job and private life.

If you want to reorient yourself professionally, you need to have a clear objective and know how to reach it. Take an example from the athletes: Before they run off mindlessly towards their goal, they get an overview and make sure they have the right equipment. Their preparation includes all five levels: Body, emotions, "Inner Fire", understanding, and spirit. The most successful is the one who has paid attention to all five.

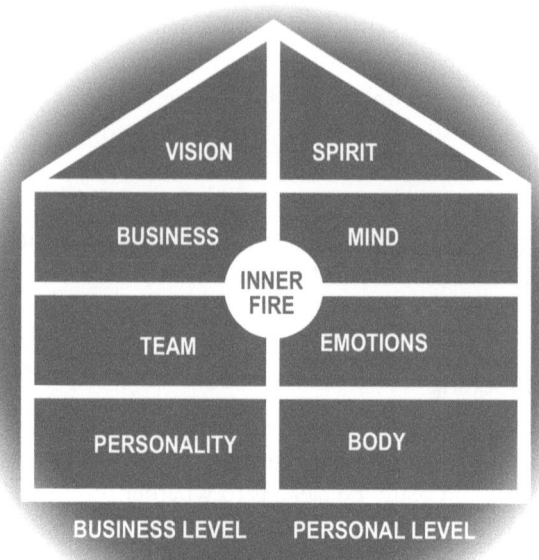

As a first step, take a deeper look at your personality. The path to success lies through these three questions:
- Who Am I?
- What can I do?
- Where do I want to go?

Who Am I?

Don't be satisfied with the tip of the iceberg – take a deeper look and discover hidden aspects. The following self-reflection provides an opportunity for deeper self-knowledge. You can also ask a trusted person to answer the following questions. Compare your own and other's assessment.

Procedure:
1. Assume a comfortable position sitting or lying down. Turn off all sources of interruption (e.g., cell phone, telephone) so that you will not be disturbed.
2. Close your eyes and concentrate on your breath. As you inhale, your abdomen rises, and as you exhale, it sinks. Follow your breath flow with your thoughts and leave your worries behind you.
3. Imagine a house. The house represents your personality with all its parts: The ground floor of the house is your body. It represents stability and security. The second floor symbolizes your emotions and social competence. Your "Inner Fire" dwells on the third floor. Your heart's desires and, as the name implies, your "Inner Fire" that drives and motivates you, are found here. Your understanding is on the fourth floor. In this area, you develop concepts and analyze your situation. If you are overwhelmed in this area, it would be wise to make some space and let in some fresh air. You develop your visions and goals in the attic. This is where you spirit dwells.
4. Discover which level (floor) you feel most comfortable and "at home" on. Which level should you pay more attention to for your professional re-orientation? Are there floors that you rarely visit? Maybe you should redecorate certain areas and give them a second life?
5. Close this meditation by opening your eyes and focusing on your body and your surroundings.

What can I do?

Discover your strengths and what makes you special. You can get a first impression from a personal assessment based on the following questions:
- What are my strengths?
- What makes me unique?
- What would I do, if I could do anything in the world?
- What comes easily to me?

Where do I want to go?

Discover what you truly want. What makes you happy and satisfied? Goals are like lights in the darkness that show us the way. They give you the motivation you need on your journey.

The following questions can help you determine your goals:
- Do I like my job? If not, what should be different?
- What did I want to be/do, when I was a teenager?
- What job would I really like to have? What field would I like to work in?
- What job advertisements appeal to me?

Motivation Leads to the Goal

Whether personal or professional, the most important first steps to change are your visions and goals. Write them down. Then start planning. You will constantly need motivation on the way to your visions and goals. So pay attention to your well-being until your ideas have finally been realized and you can look back with satisfaction.

Successful Personalities

Successful personalities are charismatic people. They convince others with their ideas, actions, and being. They are authentic people who are true to themselves. They have a powerful charm that draws others in and carries them along. If someone is not feeling well, they can hardly motivate others. It's true: Like attracts like. If you want to be a success, you should surround yourself with successful people, because success is contagious. So ask yourself if you are surrounding yourself with people and situations that are good for you. What gives you energy? You need energy for change. So take care that your batteries are always being charged. Create a life with people and situations that match your own.

That might mean you have to cut ties with old acquaintances or let go of old habits. Trust your heart and your inner voice. They are your constant companions who will show you the way. Listen to them and be honest with those around you, even when it's hard. Remember: Practice makes perfect. Small children can show you how. They are so honest that it sometimes embarrasses their parents. They are pure light. They are the clarity that grownups need to relearn. Walk with self-confidence and self-trust through the world and you will be able to experience much joy and many beautiful experiences. You will attract "like".

Stumbling blocks along the way are challenges that you should view as learning experiences. Focus your attention on what you want. Let others "be". Accept challenges with your whole heart; in this way, they will decrease in hardship. They dissolve at the right time: When you have learned the lesson. Maybe you are already so far advanced that it's only your mind tricking you into thinking that something is wrong. Learn to distinguish between your understanding and your higher consciousness. Use your mind only for the things that it was intended for. It is an expert in planning, organizing, and structuring. Let it work in the right places. In this way, you will find *your* chosen place, the place you have chosen. Always listen to the message that your heart chakra sends you. Your heart consciousness is always perfectly clear and has the whole picture in view.

Summer

Are you in summer? Then take care to always feed your motivation. Revisit your visions and goals from time to time. Trust that they will be realized. Maybe you want to complete another Goal Programming (see chapter: What are my visions?). It is useful when you want to call up your target image before your inner eye, or write it down and read through it again and again. You can also create a motivational sentence that you tape on the bathroom mirror.

You can support your motivation and endurance with scents, such as essential oils of mandarin, cinnamon, or vanilla. Colors can also stimulate you. Choose a strong orange or yellow. The color pink also has a strengthening effect. Pay attention to your sense of well-being as you choose your colors. Which color speaks to you right now; which colors make you feel good? Buy clothes, bath towels, or paint pictures with these colors. Be creative. Choose whatever speaks to you.

Fall

Fall is the time of harvest. Now is the time to think about your skills and the projects you have completed, the projects you can be proud of. What have you achieved so far in your life? What things do you deserve a pat on the back for? Take a moment and think about what fruit you can now harvest. Be proud of yourself and your accomplishments. Be thankful for your life. It is worth living and should be enjoyed to the fullest. Live NOW. Also consider how you might bring more variety into your daily life. Enjoy your life to the fullest.

Winter

Slow down instead of burning out. In the economy, winter is often neglected and scorned. But it is important to know that something new can only come when there is enough strength available. A car cannot be driven without interruption to infinity. It needs to be refueled and turned off so that it can cool down.

The more we learn to make space for winter and consciously live through these periods from time to time, the more strength we will have to accomplish great things. Today there are companies who have recognized this and have decided to give their employees a half-day off. They know that sometimes the best ideas come out of this so-called free time.

In this turbulent time in the world, it is even more important to schedule time for quiet moments. The major changes within and without demand more energy, and need to be assimilated and processed. The physical body needs lots of rest and relaxation, especially in times of growth. The approaching spiritual processes want to be anchored in the material, i.e., in the physical body.

People who are suffering from fatigue should be aware that this is a natural symptom of change and growth. Take the time you need and plan quiet moments into your daily schedule. Even a power nap in the afternoon can work wonders; and a five-minute meditation is good for all levels of your being.

In times of uncertainty, change, and awakening, everyone needs a lot of strength and motivation. Sometimes it is difficult to recharge or release pent-up energy in the midst of daily life. The answer is quiet and relaxation. But how and where? Make meditation a daily habit, choosing of one of the meditations in this book, such as the Tree Meditation, Rainbow Breathing, Heart Meditation, or Goal Programming. They will help you cope with your daily life more easily and in a relaxed mood. The business meditations help to recharge your personal batteries with new energy, serenity, and concentration. I call them business meditations because they are so short. They offer a path to more efficiency, satisfaction, and overall well-being. You will gain distance from professional stressors and reveal personal things in your world today. Then, you can see the issue with a new perspective and approach problems and difficulties in a much more relaxed way. They lose their importance and you can easily let them go. In western countries, meditation is mostly practiced as a method to deal with stress and to support one's overall well-being. In the East and with indigenous peoples, it is a philosophy of life.

The business meditation begins at the moment you turn your entire attention to the present, to the "now". It can be practiced with your eyes open or closed. Business meditations bring the following benefits:

- Brings work-life balance
- Centers and strengthens your personal center
- Recharges your energy
- Relaxes you
- Increases self-knowledge
- Develops your personality and potential
- Grows your self-awareness and self-trust

EXERCISE: Basic Meditation

The basic meditation is a deep, conscious belly breath. It is the foundation for every kind of relaxation. A deep and conscious breath brings the body new oxygen. The inhalation provides they body with new power and the exhale helps to release obstructions (also emotional). Baggage can be consciously released with repeated, long, deliberate exhales. The basic meditation balances, revitalizes, and calms. You can find guided meditations in the shop on my Homepage: www.bernardi.li

Procedure:
1. Assume a comfortable position sitting or lying down. Turn off all sources of interruption (e.g., cell phone, telephone) so that you will not be disturbed.
2. Close your eyes and concentrate on your breath. As you inhale, your abdomen rises, and as you exhale, it sinks. Follow the breath flow with your thoughts and direct your thoughts completely inward. If other thoughts come up, imagine they are clouds. Let them pass through you. You continue to breathe deeply and calmly, in and out.
3. After a while, imagine that you are taking in new strength and inspiration with every new breath (inhale) and releasing everything that burdens you with every release (exhale).
4. Remain in this exercise until you are completely relaxed. Open your eyes and focus your attention on your body and your surroundings.

Tip: Everyday Quiet and Relaxation

The following tips will help you find more quiet time and relaxation in your daily life:
- **Create free space**
  How can new ideas surface when your schedule is already full of appointments and leaves no room for a quiet minute? Deliberately leave space for new ideas and impulses. For example, mark off a few hours every Friday morning to develop inspiration, brainstorm ideas, and have some time alone. Keep your door shut and let calls go to voice mail.
- **Take time off and enjoy it!**
  Everyone needs a least one day for re-creation. Athletes always plan rest periods into their training schedules and do not train every day. Enjoy the weekend with your loved ones and leave your day planner and cell phone at home.
- **What you do, do right**
  Set your priorities and do one thing after the other. When you're drafting an offer or writing up a concept, do just that and nothing else. You will save time and nerves when you check your emails only one time/day. Who says that we need to be accessible at all times? This is often just a personal expectation.
- **Play relaxing music in the background**
  We become more relaxed when there is relaxing background music while we are working. This alpha state is conducive to more creativity and peace, since both the right and left halves of the brain are simultaneously active. In an alert state, only the left half of the brain is active. That is why it is difficult to produce good ideas on command.

EXERCISE: Targeted Exercises for more Peace and Relaxation in Your Daily Life

- **Walking or Jogging Meditation**
  Take a walk or jog in nature. As you set out, leave daily concerns and bothersome thoughts behind you. Concentrate on your breath as you walk or jog, by inhaling and exhaling evenly through your nose. Inhale with every right step, for example, skipping steps according to your speed. Choose a walking/jogging speed that allows you to comfortably carry on a conversation.
- **Relaxational Writing**
  Sit down for ten minutes with a writing utensil and a piece of paper. Make sure you will be undisturbed for this time. Before you begin writing, think about what themes you want to focus on, or where you need creative input. Activate your inspiration by asking questions related to your theme, e.g.: What can I do to experience my daily life in a more relaxed and serene way? Write down everything that comes to mind. Turn off your rational brain for a moment. Every idea is welcome. Just as in brainstorming, everything is allowed and nothing is criticized. The relaxational writing can also be helpful with themes that are weighing on you and that won't give you any peace. It could be a difficult client or a fight with your partner at home. In this case, write a letter to that person that you will not send. Write down everything that is worrying or bothering you about that person or the situation. When you are done, ask yourself what this situation could be teaching you. Because everything in your life that somehow affects you has something to do with you. Maybe you should learn a new way to deal with situations like this or to remove yourself from such situations. Does it have a message for you? Close your letter by thanking the other person. Every conflict and every situation like this is an opportunity for you to further evolve.

- **Sleep and power naps**
  Sleep is a wonderful opportunity for your body to relax on all levels and for you to recuperate. Lying down relaxes your brain, and you feel fresh and invigorated when you wake. If possible, you should schedule 30min in the afternoon. Set your alarm to make sure you wake.
- **Empty Head**
  Someone who has to work a lot mentally throughout the day may sometimes have difficulties, after a while, to form clear or new thoughts. At some point, it's just too much. Moreover, he is so focused on thoughts that he cannot be open to new ideas. A simple exercise that can be done anywhere can help: Hold your forehead with one hand and the back of your head with the other. Do not apply pressure; just lightly touch your head with your hands. Close your eyes and breathe deeply. Open your eyes when your head has stilled. Some people may feel a pleasant coolness on their forehead after doing this exercise.
- **Work-Life Balance**
  A human being consists of body, mind, and soul. Every part should be distinctly observed and cared for. Are you so busy with brainwork all day that you don't have time for your personal needs and desires? Are you always outward-focused? Take an evening to relax, enjoy a romantic candlelight dinner, or get away for a spa weekend.
  Take care of your body. Eat healthily, drink water, and use your body by jogging or swimming at a comfortable pace (where you can still carry on a conversation). Gardening or going for a stroll are also good for your body.

To Do

This is a list of concrete steps that will help you reach your goal and develop your potential. Compare the season you chose with reality. Your choice represents your SHOULD-BE situation; the reality your IS situation. This should show you which themes are important for you now and what you should bring more of into your life.

Come up with some specific actions you can take now to shift from your IS situation to your SHOULD-BE situation. The Tips and Tricks mentioned above will help you with this. Maybe you will also think of some other ways to develop your potential.

Questions for personal reflection:
1. Where am I personally and professionally?
2. Does this match to where I would like to be?
3. How can I better integrate my personal rhythm into my daily life?
4. What should I be expressing/experiencing more of right now?
5. How can I best live up to my personal rhythm?

Possible steps to better live your personal rhythm:
- **Spring**
  Start a new project, start out on a new path, and begin something new
- **Summer**
  Develop projects and follow through with strength of will, endure
- **Fall**
  Write down things you can be proud of. What is your harvest?
- **Winter**
  Retreat, personal reflection, find closure for old, completed projects/people/things, stillness and re-creation

Personal Insights

At the end of this exercise or before you go to bed, take a moment and answer the following questions spontaneously:
- What personal insights do I take from this exercise?
- What points will I follow in the future?
- When will I begin to apply these insights?

Chakras – Recognize Your Energy Levels

Many test methods on the market measure hard factors, such as a person's professional competence, although a resume provides enough information. In personal and professional development processes, however, the soft factors that make up the uniqueness of human beings are important. Holistically oriented, projective test methods help people recognize and understand their personality as a whole. The tests in this book belong to this category. They are based on images. They are hard to predict or manipulate and are therefore quite objective.

Intuitive test procedures, such as the chakra balance, offer you the opportunity to let your subconscious mind speak to you. Because the test subject doesn't know what is being analyzed or how, intuitive procedures based on colors and symbols are hard to influence. Moreover, these exercises reveal deep-lying issues that can hardly be detected and brought into consciousness with conventional test questions.

When using chakra analysis, as with all the other tests in this book, it is important that you perform the exercises without forethought and that you listen to your first impulse. Pay attention to the first signals that may come to you as an inner voice, inner images, or a feeling.

Self-test: Chakras

Color the seven circles and four connecting lines impulsively.

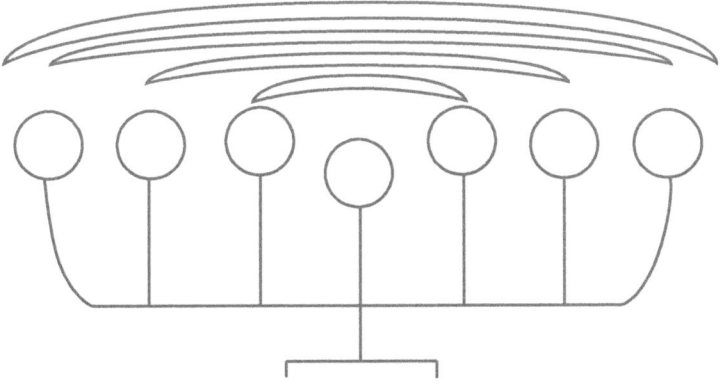

Meaning of the Chakras

A human being is comparable to a power plant. He produces energy and exchanges it with his environment. We have seven main energy centers (chakras). These are located equidistant from the coccyx to the top of the head (fontanelle). They have various functions. Furthermore, each chakra is associated with a specific color.

The word chakra comes from the Sanskrit (ancient Indian language) and means "wheel". The chakras connect your subtle with your physical body. They are your personal energy centers, where your individual themes are stored.

The chakra-balance reveals your chakra profile. Each color, in combination with its respective chakra, tells you something about your personality. That is why the colors that you chose do not have to be the same as the classical chakra colors. You can recognize even more potential, possible blockages, and how you are balanced. You can see where you can begin to develop your potential holistically.

The use of the colors black and grey, and all other dark colors in the chakra balance indicate blockages. Bright, light colors show that the chakras and connections are functioning harmonically. Blocked chakras cannot optimally develop their potential. Stopped up connections lead to bad communication between the individual energy centers. They indicate disharmony in the energetic areas of the body. A completely evolved person has harmonically flowing chakras and connecting lines. Only in this way can he optimally use his full potential.

The following list of positions in the body and functions of the individual chakras should help you to recognize and understand your personal themes and current processes. Read through the meanings and effects of the individual chakras and relate this to yourself. Pay special attention to the chakras that, according to your chakra-balance, are blocked and are not currently using or experiencing the full potential of the energy center.

Every chakra has a different position and function in the body:

- **Root chakra (first circle from the left in the Chakra Balance Exercise)**
  Position: The first energy center lies between the anus and the genitals and is connected with the tailbone.
  Classic chakra color: Red
  Harmonic function: If this area is in balance, you will feel secure, stable, and full of vitality. You stand with both legs firmly on the floor. Moreover, you are satisfied and feel a basic sense of trust.
  Dissonant function: Your thinking and behaviors are limited to material possessions and security. Letting go is difficult. You are attached to the past.
  Ideas need grounding, so it is important to stand with both legs on the earth. A conscious walk through nature or playing sports can balance this center.

- **Sacral chakra (second circle from the left in the Chakra Balance Exercise)**
  Position: The second center is located near the belly button. It is connected with the sacrum.
  Classical chakra color: Orange
  Harmonic function: If this center is in balance, your interpersonal partnerships will be harmonic. Giving and taking are balanced.
  Dissonant function: In dissonance, a person will continually enter into personal or vocational partnerships that are not right for them. This leads to insecurities and tension.
  Students often find themselves on this plane during their course of study. It has to do with the receiving, processing, and delivering of subject matter. Work relationships also fall into this area. An employee gives services and ideas to a business in return for pay. It is important that the give and take be balanced and that the situation be win-win. Clarifying the question of appreciated value (i.e., how much a person receives on the

material plane for his or her work) has a harmonizing effect on the second energy center. The question of value and balance is important to the success of every type of partnership.

- **Solar plexus (third circle on the left in the Chakra Balance Exercise)**
  Position: The third energy center is located beneath the costal arch, between the end of the breastbone and the belly button.
  Classical chakra color: Yellow
  Harmonic function: If this area is in balance, you will feel power and vitality. You honor your own and other people's feelings and idiosyncrasies and accept them as they are.
  Dissonant function: If this area is not in balance, a person tends to be manipulative. He or she uses power to try and control everything to their personal interest.
  The third energy center is your center of power. It is your inner sun. Conscious and prescribed sunbathing has a harmonizing effect on this area. Excessive sunbathing has the opposite effect.

- **Heart chakra (middle circle in the Chakra Balance Exercise)**
  Position: The fourth energy center lies at the level of your heart, in the center of your chest.
  Classical chakra color: Green
  Harmonic function: If this area is in balance, love for and harmony with yourself and others will flow outward. People and animals tend to feel comfortable in your presence.
  Dissonant function: If this area is closed, the person will isolate himself from others. Because of this protective wall, he comes across as reserved and cool.
  Managers tend to be stuck in this area. It is a form of self-protection that nevertheless also separates you from yourself. You can balance this aspect through unconditional devotion and openness in a partnership. Love can heal everything. Research has shown that sick people who receive a great deal of love heal faster than others.

- **Throat chakra (third circle from the right in the Chakra Balance Exercise)**
  Position: The fifth energy center is located between the base of the throat and the larynx and is connected with the neck.
  Classical chakra color: Blue
  Harmonic function: If this area is in balance, the person is expressive, communicative, and creative. Moreover, he possesses a personalized form of expression.
  Dissonant function: In dissonance, it is difficult for the person to communicate his/her feelings and thoughts. Dammed-up emotions will be let out in an uncontrolled fashion.
  The development of this energy center is important, especially in the areas of marketing and sales. If a person has to clear his or her throat or if he feels a scratching in the throat, this is often an indication that something needs to be communicated. Writing down one's personal feelings, thoughts, and visions has a harmonizing effect on this energy center. Gazing at the radiant blue sky brings the throat area into balance.

- **Third eye (second circle from the right in the Chakra-Balance Exercise)**
  Position: The sixth energy center is located between the eyebrows, where Hindu women wear a bindi.
  Classical chakra color: Violet
  Harmonic function: If this energy center is in balance, the person has a sharp mind and is a clear thinker. He is often highly visual and can make his goals and visions a reality through mental powers.
  Dissonant function: If this plane is not in harmony, the person is "top-heavy" (i.e., overly-intellectual). He lives in his mind and tries to control everything on this plane.
  Managers are often "top-heavy" and try to experience their feelings through their intellect. Immersing oneself in a bubble bath or consciously enjoying a massage brings the sixth energy center into balance. The mental and emotional planes can be connected and brought into balance by holding your forehead with one hand and your bellybutton with the other.

- **Crown chakra (first circle on the right in the Chakra Balance Exercise)**
  Position: The seventh energy center is located at the crown of the head, at the top of the fontanel.
  Classical chakra color: White
  Harmonic function: If this area is developed, the person is innovative and full of ideas.
  Dissonant function: If this area is under-developed, the person lacks a holistic viewpoint.
  Ideas have their origin in this area. As already mentioned, you can visualize this opening that the energy pours into like a funnel. The wider the opening, the more inspiration the person will receive.

Tips and Tricks

Chakra Energy Balance

The Chakra Balance is a good start to energetically balance the 7 main chakras. Through it, you (or your client) will have an insight into the current state of the chakras. You can then balance the individual chakras and connections with each other through energy equilibration using the hands.

The Chakra Energy Balance is also a good exercise to do in bed before you get up or fall asleep to harmonize all 7 main chakras. Children also enjoy this exercise as a good-night ritual.

Procedure:
1. Turn off all sources of interruption (e.g., cell phone, telephone) so that you will not be disturbed. Play some relaxing music in the background. You can light some incense or a scent-lamp with a favorite scent. Lie comfortably. Close your eyes and breathe deeply in and out through your nose.

2. After some time, rest both hands on the chakra that you want to balance. Imagine that strength and healing from the Source is flowing through your hands into this energy center. You can also let light and love from the Source stream in. Remain in this position until you have a comfortable feeling in this area. Maybe you will feel some warmth or a slight tickling. This lets you know that the energy stream is flowing harmoniously.
3. Complete step 2 for all the chakras that are blocked, according to the Chakra Balance. You can also take a little more time and lay your hands on all your chakras, from root to crown.
4. Concentrate next on the blocked connecting lines in your Chakra Balance. Equalize the energy by laying your hands on the chakras connected by the blocked line (e.g., crown-root chakras; sacral-third eye chakras; solar plexus-throat chakras). Breathe light and love from the Source through your hands into these chakras to balance. You can also imagine power flowing in through your hands. Remain in the exercise until you have the sense that the work is complete. Continue in the same way with all the various connecting lines that you want to balance.
5. At the end of the Chakra Energy Balance, rest there for a moment and sense the effect of this energy work. How are you doing? How do you feel? Take the power of this balance with you in your daily life. Do this exercise whenever you feel that you are out of balance. Your body is like a seismograph; it tells you when it wants to be balanced. Of course, for energy balancing you can certainly go to a professional or ask your partner to help you. The Chakra Energy Balance is a wonderful exercise to invest in the connection and depth of your partnership.

Try the Chakra Energy Balance. Trust in your personal ability to heal. Every person carries this power in them.

Chakra Balance Breath

Do this exercise whenever you want to do something good for yourself. At the beginning, it might seem a little strange to do an exercise like this. But with time, you will see that you feel better and better with this balance. The warmth (the healing energy) of your hands will also increase. The more it is used and the more you trust it, the more it flows. Be thankful for this gift. Give yourself devotion and love through this exercise.

Through the Chakra Balance Breath, you balance the seven energy centers. You will be calmer, centered, have more vitality, health, and well-being.

Procedure:
1. Turn off all sources of interruption (e.g., cell phone, telephone) so that you will not be disturbed. Play some relaxing music in the background. Lie comfortably. Close your eyes and breathe deeply in and out through your nose.
2. After a little time, rest both hands on your root chakra. Breathe deeply in and out through this chakra. As you inhale, the power in the area reaches out from this area in your body like a spiral. As you exhale, draw the spiral back into your body, back into the energy center. Imagine that you are letting power and healing flow into this energy center. You can also let light and love from the Source flow in.
3. After some time, continue with the next chakra as in step 2. You can proceed with the Chakra Balance Breath from bottom to top, or from top to bottom.

To Do

Your Chakra Balance reveals subconscious themes and blockages. Compare these with your reality. Consider what specific actions you can use to balance your chakras. The above-mentioned tips and tricks will help you. Maybe you will also think of some other possibilities to balance your chakras.

Questions for personal reflection:
1. What are my personal insights from the Chakra Balance?
2. What tips and tricks will I continue to use?
3. What effects will my insights from the Chakra Balance have on my life?
4. Am I aware of the open and blocked chakras in my daily life?
5. What will I start doing today to regularly balance my chakras?
6. How can I integrate the wisdom of the chakras and the meaning of the individual chakras in my life?
7. Which chakras did I color with dark colors? What effect does that have for me? What will I do to balance these?
8. What do my blocked chakras want to tell me? As you consider this, consider the meaning of the individual chakras.
9. What do I especially notice when I consider the allocation of colors to the individual chakras?

Possible actions to harmonize your chakras:
- **Crown chakra**
  Stand under the open sky and gaze at the sun. You can also imagine the sun. Let the power of the sun, the gold-yellow rays, stream into your body. Recharge on the light of the sun on your skin and let it flow into your physical body. Stream the sunlight into every cell, every pore, and every part of your physical body. Concentrate especially on the dark places that you sense or detect with your inner eye. Let the energy of the sun flow into these areas until they are bright. If you do not perceive any dark places, then listen to your inner voice as it tells you where they are, or trust your feeling. Creative activities also encourage the energy flow in the crown chakra. Allow your creative vein to flow into an activity or a project. Let yourself be inspired by this work and immerse yourself totally in it. You can give voice to your creativity by painting, doing pottery, imagining things and writing them

down. There are limitless possibilities. Concentrate on something that brings you joy. Maybe you want to sew your next curtains yourself!

- **Third Eye**

  Hold your forehead and the back of your head as described in the Stress Reduction Exercise in this book. This exercise clears the understanding and helps stop the hamster wheel in your head. Mountain crystals have a clear and pure energy. Buy yourself a stone that speaks to you and, before you fall asleep, lay the stone on your forehead. Amethysts are soothing and calming. They balance the third eye.

  Treatments by spiritual teachers, kinesiologists, and healers who can stimulate the head point are well-suited for balancing the head area. Managers especially enjoy the laying on of hands onto their heads by healers. When you are selecting outside help, it is important that you feel some chemistry with the spiritual leader which will help you choose the right one. You can get a first impression from their website, photo, business card, or resume. You should listen to your intuition when making your choice. Choose someone who speaks to you.

  If you like scents, buy 100% essential lavender oil. Take a few drops on your hand and smell it a few times. Breathe the relaxing perfume deeply.

  You can also stroke your forehead. Rub your fingers from your third eye up to your hairline.

- **Throat Chakra**

  The throat chakra is the energy center of expression, of communication. Singing and speaking stimulate this chakra. Stand up for who you are and give it voice. Express yourself and communicate your desires and needs. Take up your space. Buy and carry in your pant or jacket pocket a light-blue stone. Carry this stone with you whenever you have important discussions or presentations. It will bring you a smoother speech flow and increase your powers of expression. Let yourself be counseled in a stone store or choose one instinctively.

- **Heart Chakra**
  Do the Heart Meditation from the chapter: "What is my Mission?". It promotes self-love, strengthens your personal center, and helps you balance your heart chakra. The more you listen to your heart in all decisions, the more harmonically the energy will flow into your heart chakra. Experience joy in nature, from a green field or a single tree. Consciously take in this power and joy. You will feel your heart open and fill with warmth. Even if you don't perceive anything, trust the effect. Babies and small children also open our hearts. Wear light pink, green, or pink clothing. They also stimulate your heart chakra and have a beneficial effect.
- **Solar plexus**
  Your strength and power centers lie in your solar plexus. It holds all themes having to do with power. To balance this center, renounce pressure-based discussions or exchanges. Renounce expressions of power. Let your counterpart have his way and set boundaries where necessary, in love. Ideally, you will find a common thread and won't need to compromise. If you have a position of influence or are an influential personality, use your power for the greater good. Let a golden sun spin in your solar plexus. If this area is blocked, then it will spin first counter clockwise and then clockwise. Trust your body-feeling or the results of the Chakra Balance to assess this. Let the rays stream through all your physical and subtle bodies.
- **Sacral chakra**
  People who have not yet harmonized this area should ask themselves the following question: Are the situations that I create with others win-win? Do I give more than I receive? Stomach massages are beneficial for the sacral chakra. You should also pay close attention to maintaining a balanced diet so that the pH balance is optimized. PH test strips to test the pH of your urine are available at the drug store. Base powders, cleansing tees, and baking soda are also balancing. A deep, conscious belly breath helps the energy flow to balance

down to the root chakra. Insert a golden ball in your belly button. This will protect you from belly heaviness. You will learn to communicate with others through the heart chakra.
- **Root chakra** People who aren't grounded can strengthen their root chakra and their physical bodies with moderate sports such as jogging, walking, and light strength training. It is worthwhile to go barefoot on Mother Earth as often as possible. Cool footbaths in the shower or in a stream draw the energy down into the feet. Red underwear, socks, or painted toenails ground and strengthen the root chakra. Pelvic floor training, such as Pilates, can also work wonders.

The root chakra may also be strengthened through connection with Mother Earth. Imagine the power of the earth, her light and her love, streaming in through the soles of your feet. Let this energy flow through every cell, every pore, and every part of your physical body. Concentrate especially on the dark parts that your inner eye perceives. Let the energy of Mother Earth flow in until these parts are light. If you cannot perceive any dark places, listen to your inner voice to direct you to the appropriate area and trust your feeling.

Personal Insights

At the end of this exercise or before you go to bed, take a moment and answer the following questions intuitively:
- What personal insights can I take from this exercise?
- What points will I develop in the future?
- When will I begin to apply these insights?

Rainbow Breathing – Create Personal Balance

Rainbow Breathing is a mental exercise that balances the physical and etheric bodies through the chakras (energy centers). The colors of the rainbow offer connections to the chakras. They recreate, completely naturally, the energetic balance of the body. The effect of the color spectrum of the rainbow can range from relaxing to energizing. Balance is thereby reestablished. Rainbow Breathing can be done as a short-term relaxation to release tension or can help you to fall and stay asleep.

Moreover, a rainbow is a visual opportunity to be present with yourself. Take a few seconds before you go into a shopping center or are confronted with uncomfortable people or situations to imagine a rainbow over your head. This will help you stay present with yourself.

Test the effect of this meditation. Use the rainbow deliberately in your life.

Procedure:
1. Assume a comfortable position, sitting or lying down. Turn off all sources of disturbance, e.g., cell phones, telephones, etc., so that you won't be interrupted.
2. Close your eyes; inhale and exhale deeply through your nose. Place both hands on your bellybutton. Feel how your abdomen rises as you inhale and sinks as you exhale. Follow the breath-flow with your thoughts. If other thoughts come up, let them pass through like clouds across the sky. Thoughts come and go. Let them go.
3. Imagine you are inhaling new strength and motivation with every inhale and with every exhale, releasing everything old, heavy, and burdensome. Leave your troubles behind you with every exhaled breath. With every release, you become more calm and relaxed. You become more and more deeply re-

laxed. Follow your breath with your thoughts until you are completely relaxed.
4. Imagine a rainbow over your head. Breathe the colors of the rainbow deliberately into your physical body. With every exhalation, allow these colors to spread through every cell, every pore, and every part of your physical body. Nourish your body with the power of the colors of the rainbow. Consciously feel the power of this meditation. The meditation is also effective when you don't consciously feel its power.
5. Instinctively choose a color that attracts you. Breathe this color deliberately into your physical body and allow it to spread with every exhaled breath. Stain every cell, every part of your body with this color. Travel through your body with your thoughts and guide this color from your head to the tips of your fingers and toes.
6. Extend this color over your physical body. Create a sphere around yourself. This sphere is your aura, your charisma. Fill this sphere completely with the color you selected, so that there isn't room for anything else.
7. Make contact with the rainbow over your head again by taking a few deep, conscious breaths. Open your eyes when you feel ready. Carry the balance from the Rainbow Breathing Meditation with you into your day.

WHAT IS MY MISSION?

The soul's mission is, for some people, very soft, and for others, easier to hear. But every one of us needs courage to be able to follow our soul's mission. It's a leap of faith. If you follow your inner impulse and dare to take a step into the unknown, endless power will be released. You will feel freed and satisfied. Moreover, you will feel centered and strengthened in your core. You can use the energy that you have gained for the projects to come.

A person who has realized their mission is secure and centered in their personal center. The exercises in this section will help you achieve that. When the time is ripe, you will have the possibility of realizing the call of your soul and find your way to your true mission. How do they say? "Time will tell." That's how it is with your personal path of development. Everything comes at the right time and you will become aware of it at the right time. Spontaneous healings also happen this way. When it is the right time, the healer is the medium that will bring success. So trust that the following exercises will show you what is important for you now. Have patience and persevere.

Heart Meditation – Strengthen Your Personal Center

The Heart Meditation is a lovely and relaxed method to strengthen your personal center, to find yourself, and to develop your personal potential. Discover the great power in the middle of your heart using this Heart Meditation. Your heart chakra, in the middle of your chest, is a source full of love, peace, and well-being. Allow room for something new to arrive.

Take a break from everyday life and recharge new energy in a safe space. You will carry this space with you always. If you regularly do the meditation, it will be easier for you to embrace your strength every day. What is more, you will live more consciously from your personal middle and be centered.

It is worthwhile to listen to your heart every day. A person who is completely anchored in his center is in accord with himself and his life. He is protected and feels good in his skin. The love and purity that the heart chakra radiates is the strongest energy in the universe. You will have strong healing powers. It has been scientifically proven that people in the hospital who receive love from those close to them heal faster than others. So regularly recharge yourself with this power from your heart chakra. Be consciously aware of this energy and nourish your body with it.

Procedure:
1. Assume a comfortable position, sitting or lying down. Turn off all sources of disturbance, e.g., cell phones, telephones, etc., so that you won't be interrupted.
2. Close your eyes; inhale and exhale deeply through your nose. Place both hands on your bellybutton. Feel how your abdomen rises as you inhale and sinks as you exhale. Follow the breath-flow with your thoughts. If other thoughts come up, let them pass through like clouds across the sky. Thoughts come and go. Let them go.

3. Imagine you are inhaling new strength and motivation with every inhale and with every exhale, releasing everything old, heavy, and burdensome. Leave your troubles behind you with every exhaled breath. With every release, you become more calm and relaxed. You become increasingly relaxed. Follow your breath with your thoughts until you are completely relaxed.
4. After some time, lay both hands on your heart chakra in the middle of your chest. Focus entirely on your personal center. Inhale warmth and love in the center. As you exhale, concentrate entirely on this place in the middle of your chest. Maybe you will notice, after a time, that the spot becomes warm or that you have a pleasant feeling there. If you don't consciously sense anything, trust that the meditation's effect is unfolding below the conscious level.
5. Remain for a moment in the stillness of your heart chakra. Consciously enjoy the peace and warmth. Enjoy the moment.
6. Let the love in your heart expand outwards and spread through your entire physical body. Nourish every cell, every muscle, and every part of your physical body with your love. Smile gently to inwards to yourself. Notice how your physical body feels.
7. Spread your love over your entire physical body and imagine a sphere surrounding your body. Maybe you can even see this sphere with your inner eye. Fill the sphere with your love and feed it with this love.
8. The sphere is your personal space. If you want it to be bigger, expand it until it feels right. Rest for a moment in this expansion.
9. Close the meditation by concentrating on your heart chakra. Take a few more deep, conscious breaths and then open your eyes.

Relationship Map – Get to Know Your Inner Map

Every person has an inner map of situations, people, and other themes. This relationship map is a support method to concretize these images and to highlight subconscious dynamics and relationships. It can be used for personal and professional themes. In conflict or unclear situations, it can bring clarity.

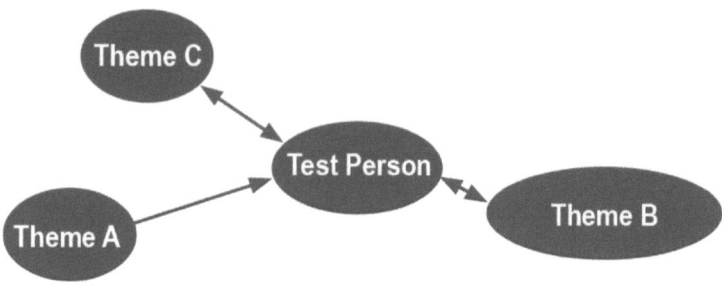

Self-Test

Take out a piece of white paper and something to write with. If you use colored pencils, you can incorporate the color symbolism in your assessment and interpretation of your relationship map.

Choose a theme or situation that you are worried about and about which you are seeking clarity. Draw this theme instinctively on the paper. Let yourself be guided by your first impulse. You can use symbols, drawings, or simply circles to represent each thematic area. Draw all the points that make up the overall picture. Also draw the relationships between the individual points. You can use lines and arrows.

When you are done, look at your picture intuitively and using the chakra graphic, which you already know from the chakra Tree of Life analysis.

Chakra Graphic

The grid with the seven main chakras helps you to assess your relationship map from a higher level. Divide your paper into seven equal quadrants. If you have drawn your relationship map in 'landscape', then label the areas from left to right. The root chakra is furthest to the right. 'Portrait' drawings are divided from bottom to top. The root chakra in these images will be at the bottom. Please note that the Relationship Map is an intuitive test process.

Trust your first impulse, your intuition in your assessment.

Assess your Relationship Map with the help of the Chakra Graphic by seeing in which chakra the various circles, symbols, or drawing are positioned. Consider the significance of the individual chakras (areas). Also consider the color symbolic in your assessment, if you used color. What significance do the colors have and where are they in your drawing? What is the corresponding chakra theme?

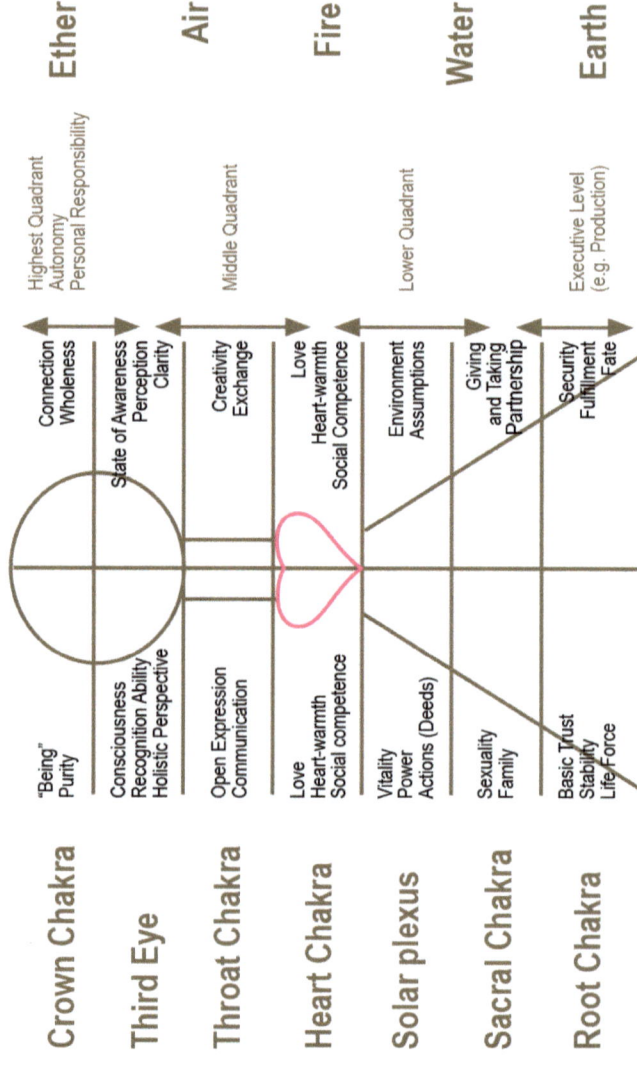

Medicine Circle

The medicine wheel, which goes back to the knowledge of the indigenous and star peoples, can also be consulted, upon request, to assess your Relationship Map.

In the medicine circle, the five elements: ether, air, fire, water, earth, are assigned various directions. The element air lays to the north, Fire to the east, Water to the south, and Earth to the west. Ether is in the middle of these four. Every element has a meaning.

The five elements are arranged on the Relationship Map as follows:
- **Ether**: Middle of the paper
- **Air**: Top of the paper
- **Fire**: Right side of the paper
- **Water**: Bottom of the paper
- **Earth**: Left side of the paper

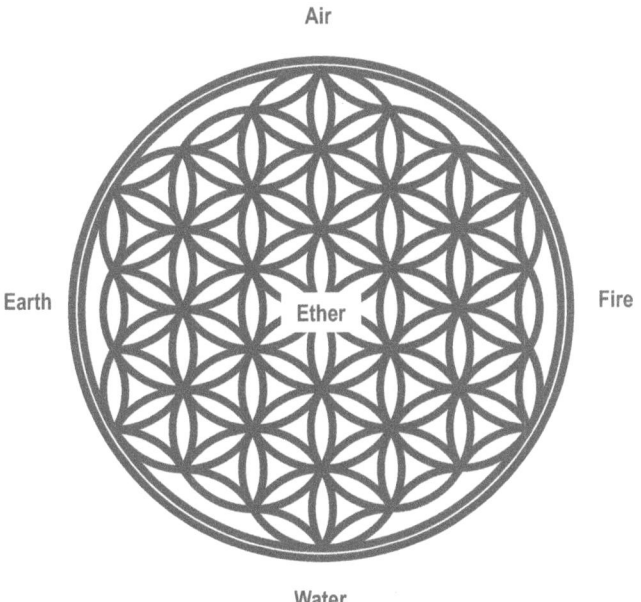

As you assess your Relationship Map, consider the significance of the placement of your circles, symbols, and/or drawings in relation to the five elements as well.

Tips and Tricks

As you are observing your Relationship Map, imagine you are observing it form a neutral position over your head. This position is also called the meta-level or higher perception. It will help you to consider your drawing from a neutral perspective. It can also be helpful to adopt this meta-level position in conflict situations. You should always try to see themes that should be perceived holistically from this perspective.

You can also show your Relationship Map to a trusted advisor or spiritual professional and ask their interpretation.

Chakra Teachings

The teachings of the chakras can be used for everything that exists on this world. They are universally applicable. Homes and gardens can also be divided according to the chakras. Interestingly, the knowledge of the chakras infiltrated old architecture, such as churches. For example, you can find circles in the ceiling of the monastery church in Einsiedeln in Switzerland that can be correlated to the individual chakras. The common people had to sit in the lowest areas (root and sacral chakras) earlier. The priests were located in the pulpit, which is the location of the third eye. This position affords great responsibility, as the church goers can be mentally directed from it. A thought-programming full of hope and faith gives the attendees strength and supports them on their way.

Is/Should Be Relationship Map

As a first step, it can be interesting to draw an "Is Situation" of a certain theme. You will receive information about the conditions and dynamics of a given theme. You can also see the interdependencies of the various people involved. After the "Is Situation", you can draw your "Wish/Future" image. After you are done drawing, think about how you can move from the "Is" to the "Should be". What can you do to realize your goal? What are your next steps?

Application of the Relationship Map

The Relationship Map can be used to clarify personal and professional themes. It can also be used to determine your standpoint and to orient your new path. It can also bring light to situations that are unclear and not easily comprehended – employer-employee conversations, for example.

Because every person has inner pictures, the application of this kind of exercise knows no bounds. It can also be interesting to observe the art work of children or artists. You can incorporate your intuition, the chakra graphic, and the color symbolism in your assessment.

Release/Healing

If the Relationship Map is rather negative, considering the colors and the overall assessment, then I strongly suggest incorporating healing directly into the drawing. Brighten the colors in the existing Relationship Map. Draw your "wish" image directly into the existing drawing until you are satisfied. Yellow and white bring especial relief and healing. Additionally, yellow brings zest and white brings cleansing. Be aware that everything that you draw is a kind of materialization, i.e., ideas will be drawn into matter on the paper.

Clothing

Everything has significance. Notice what happens when you wear various colors. The colors black and grey are limiting and protective. You can stimulate the flow of energy and lift your mood by wearing light, bright colors. You can influence your entire mood and sense of being with colors. The colored lights on the market are also based on this knowledge.

Before you get dressed, ask yourself what message you want to send with your clothes. Subconsciously, everyone receives this message. If two or more people come together, then the subconscious of these people is communicating to a large extent. The spoken word comprises only about 10% of communication and 90% of the message is nonverbal, communicated by our facial expressions, gestures, clothes, and many other subconscious and often intangible aspects of communication. The more consciously you move through life, the more clearly you can communicate. And you are not so easily influenced by others!

Evaluating the Relationship Maps with the medicine wheel can be especially interesting when the drawing depicts human relationships. It tells us in what position a person is standing and possible issues for these people. Especially in business teams and within families, it is possible to check if the position on the Relationship Map corresponds to their effective function. It comes up, time and again, that the person is in the wrong place. An accountant who is place in the element Water on the Relationship Map should ask whether or not accounting is really the right job for him. In this case, he would have a greater sense of well-being if his job offered more interaction with other people. The accounting job could bring him needed grounding, however. Accounting is connected to the Earth element.

Job correlation to the five elements:
- **Ether**: Visionaries and creative thinkers
- **Air**: Managers, planners, organizers, administrators
- **Fire**: Doers, heart-people, people who get things done
- **Water**: Social workers, people in social care jobs, HR (not including personnel administration; this falls under Earth), all jobs that have to do with interpersonal connections, e.g., nurses
- **Earth**: Accounting, controlling, management, all jobs associated with numbers and facts

Ideally, entrepreneurs, project managers, coaches, healers, teachers, and mothers merge all the elements. These people have the ability to feel at home on every level.

To Do

Your Relationship Map shows the inner picture of your current situation. It is a snapshot and shows you the "Is". This drawing can help you better understand your situation and present you with your scope of action.

Questions for personal reflection:
- Where am I in my Relationship Map?
- Does this position match to my actual position in this issue?
- Have I drawn some circles larger (i.e., more dominant) than others?
- Which colors did I assign the various circles and their connections to one another?
- Did I place the theme in the middle of the paper? (The middle of the paper symbolizes the heart, the core of the issue.)
- Did I draw any of the connections with thunder bolts (which represent tension)? If yes, what does that tell me?
- Do the arrows in your drawing point in one direction/to one person, or do they point in both directions?
- Do the connections make sense in relation to each other in terms of dynamic and interaction?

Possible actions to develop the image of the situation as shown in your Relationship Map:
1. One possibility to get an overview of the "Is" and "Should Be" situations and to develop actions is listed under Tips and Tricks.
2. Because every Relationship Map is individual, it is not possible to list general actions and possibilities for development here. Develop your own and trust their effectiveness.

Personal Insights

At the end of this exercise or before you go to bed, take a moment and answer the following questions intuitively:
- What personal insights can I take from this exercise?
- What points will I develop in the future?
- When will I begin to apply these insights?

Shamanic Timeline Journey – Mission Made Conscious

The indigenous peoples of this earth transmit knowledge from generation to generation. This knowledge is thousands of years old and contains treasures that also offer strength to the western world on its path of growth. Knowledge becomes wisdom when people apply these teachings to themselves and integrate these insights into their lives.

Every person comes to the earth with certain missions, unique abilities, and potential. This potential and these abilities support us in fulfilling our missions. Sometimes, we intuitively sense what our mission is. Realizing our mission brings great joy and motivation. We grow according to our responsibilities and are happy in that growth. The work becomes self-realization. The Shamanic Timeline Journey supports you in realizing your deepest dreams and wishes and to recognize your mission. Follow the shamans' example: dream your desired future.

Self-Test: Shamanic Timeline Journey

Complete the exercise as follows:
1. Create a timeline for yourself by laying a long string or cord on the ground. Determine for yourself where this timeline begins and ends. The timeline begins with your conception and ends with your death. Title five pages as follows, using one title per page: Mission, Possibility 1, Possibility 2, Possibility 3, Impossible. The Impossible stands for additional possibilities, since nothing is impossible.
2. Assume a comfortable position, sitting or lying down. Turn off all sources of disturbance, e.g., cell phones, telephones, etc., so that you won't be interrupted. Close your eyes; inhale and exhale deeply through your nose. Follow the breath-

flow with your thoughts. If other thoughts come up, let them pass through like clouds across the sky. Thoughts come and go. Let them go.
3. When your mind has become calm and clear, take one of the pages in your hand. Stand at the beginning of your timeline and place the paper instinctively in front of you on the ground. Do not look at what is written on the paper. Place it according to your first impulse. If you think about it for longer than 30 seconds, your mind will take over. Trust your first impulse.
4. Continue in this way with all the pages until they have all been placed.
5. Stand on one of the papers, looking towards the end of your timeline. Close your eyes. Lay both hands on your heart chakra in the middle of your chest. Continue concentrating on your breath. Breathe evenly and follow your breath-flow with your thoughts. Remain thus until you have completely relaxed. Now, imagine a screen in your mind's eye. You are watching a movie about the theme written on the paper you are standing on. If you are standing on Mission, you will see images that show you your mission. The information can come into your consciousness through various impulses. Pay attention to bursts of thought, images, and feelings. If you are not used to meditating, you can imagine that you are brainstorming about your mission. What ideas come to you spontaneously about your mission? Open your eyes when no new ideas come to you and write down your insights. Write down everything, without judgement. Continue in this way with every piece of paper. When you are standing on Possibilities, ask yourself what they look like? What are you doing there? What is your mission in this part of your life? You can observe the possibilities on your inner screen or through brainstorming.
6. When you have gone through all the possibilities, return consciously to the here and now by becoming aware of your body and your surroundings. Take a moment to let the insights from the Timeline Journey sink in.

Theme Journey	Meditative Realizations (Brainstorming)
Calling	
Possibility 1	
Possibility 2	
Possibility 3	
Impossibility	

Tips and Tricks

Depending on how active the right half of your brain is, it is possible that you won't see any images. The Shamanic Timeline Journey also works if you do it using brainstorming. With time and some meditation practice, the right side of your brain will become more active. The right side of the brain is the creative, intuitive part of the brain. The left half is analytical and structured.

Conditions for Success

Knowing is nothing without doing. So it is important that you incorporate and live the insights that you have gained from the Shamanic Timeline Journey in your daily life. Be the person that you are. Live and go your way. These are the truest conditions for a happy, inspiring, and satisfied life. Sometimes it takes courage to choose a new path. Gather your courage together and get to it! You are the master and creator of your own happiness.

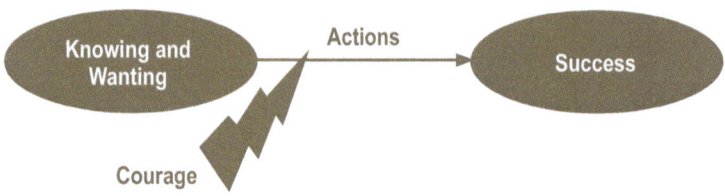

When you manage to cross that line that has, up till now, been holding you back, power and motivation are released. Your self-awareness and self-trust will be strengthened. It's just like that moment when a mountain biker tops the summit at the end of an exhausting climb. He feels amazingly victorious and as free as a bird.

Ensured Daily Application

One of the most important points to ensure that you apply these things in your daily life is the written word. Writing things down creates commitment. It is the concretization of ideas and the first step to success. Ideas that just float around in your head are easily forgotten. Let your ideas become reality and touch the ground of real life. After the ideas have been recognized, you need a tremendous amount of motivation and self-discipline. Especially when daily life and habits return, it is important for you to keep your personal desires and goals in sight.

We especially need a lot of sun, which gives us strength, on gray, rainy days. We also need to trust ourselves to follow our mission and our ideas. This can be strengthened through meditations in this book like the Heart Meditation or Rainbow Breathing. It also helps to do something that brings joy every day.

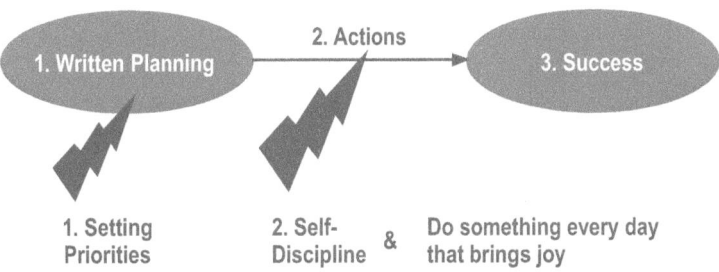

Tips for application:
- Quiet moments, i.e., empty space/free time to develop visions and new ideas
- Joy – joy in your work and your personal success makes it easier to endure
- Begin the day in a pleasant way
- Don't put off unpleasant or difficult things
- Schedule regular time for routine tasks
- Schedule set times for relaxation and physical activity

Time Management

Money and time are very important for many people in this world. Release yourself from the clock every now and again by setting your watch and/or cell phone aside. Try to consciously follow your inner rhythm. Often, less is more. Take it down a notch. Drive more slowly. Only get the most important things done. Leave unimportant things out. Cancel meetings that are not important for you.

Time Management Tips

- Organize your time wisely and effectively
- Stay realistic in your planning
- Plan in time for the unexpected (plan only 60% of your day)
- Set clear priorities
- Separate the important from the unimportant
- Regularly re-evaluate your priorities and activities
- Be consistent and flexible
- Reward yourself for your perseverance

To Dos

Think of specific actions relative to your Timeline Journey that you can do to realize your mission. The Tips and Tricks listed above will help you. You will certainly think of a few other things, as well.

Questions for personal reflection:
- By when do I want to have realized my mission?
- What do I need to do in order to live up to my mission?
- What are the next steps?
- How will I keep my motivation high during the implementation period?
- What else is keeping me from living my mission? How can I remove those blockages?

Possible actions to follow my mission are:
1. Create a schedule
2. Implement the first steps
3. Remove blockages that are in the way of my mission
4. Keep my motivation high
5. Act
6. Trust
7. Find joy in partial successes and reward myself
8. Be kind to myself, even when things are not going as I would like.

Personal Insights

At the end of this exercise or before you go to bed, take a moment and answer the following questions intuitively:
- What personal insights can I take from this exercise?
- What points will I develop in the future?
- When will I begin to apply these insights?

WHAT ARE MY VISIONS?

If you have a clear vision and goals, then you know where to direct your energy. It's like driving a taxi – the driver can bring a passenger to the right destination if he knows the destination. If you live your visions and dreams, you will be motivated and have enough strength for your daily life.

In this part of the book, you will recognize your visions and goals and recharge your motivation. Additionally, you will start setting them in motion. The most important things are your faith and perseverance. Trust that your wishes will be fulfilled.

Faith and trust can move mountains. Accept life's challenges and continue steadfastly onwards.

Project Management – Course of Action to Realize Personal Goals

Spiritual project management shows how you can manage projects in your life. It gives information about your personal management style and strategies. In this self-test, the Platonic solids represent the individual project elements. This prevents you from completing this exercise with your rational mind and helps get to the bottom of things. The Platonic solids date back to the Greek philosopher, Plato. In the Renaissance, Leonardo da Vinci incorporated this knowledge into his work. Today, the five elements form the foundation of traditional Chinese medicine.

Self-Test: Project Management

Complete the exercise as follows:
Using the five Platonic solids, think about how you approach personal projects in your life. Concentrate on a personal project. Normally, an experienced manager will use the same approach professionally as in the spiritual project management. Begin in the upper-right and going clockwise, assign a Platonic solid to every element of your project. Trust your first impulse. Read about the significance of the Platonic solids and the spiritual project management process only *after* you have completed the self-test.

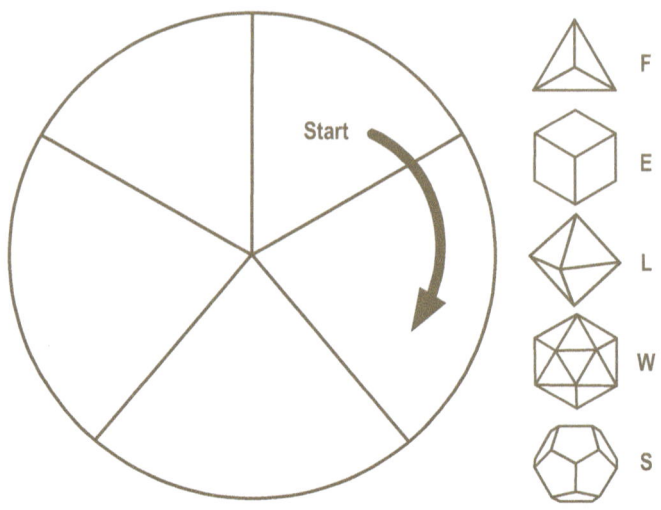

Spiritual Project Management

After you have determined your personal project management strategy, compare it with the spiritual, or holistic approach. What do you notice? Do you begin your personal projects with a clear idea/vision? At the end, do you leave space for closure, so that you can then begin the next project with zest?

Focus especially on how you begin your projects. Do you begin with a clear vision? Experience shows that many people jump into action (Element: Fire) without really knowing where they're going; or they block themselves already at the start (Element: Earth or Water).

If you want a deeper foundation for your path towards your project-goal (personal project management), then observe the sequence of the elements and if they are placed in different positions than in the spiritual project management. Do you want to continue as you have, or do you want to begin today to use these spiritual (holistic) tools? Do you have other projects that would benefit from this process?

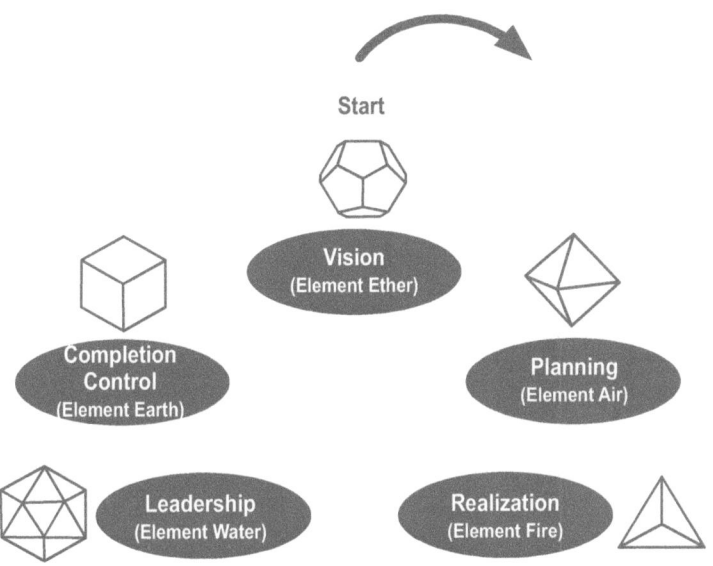

Significance of the Five Elements

The elements air, fire, water, and earth are part of earth's structure. The fifth element, ether, was described as love in the film "The Fifth Element". Element also embodies the abstract, subconscious, and invisible realms.

The five elements are associated with the following planes of your personality:
- **Spirit corresponds to Element: Ether**
  This element symbolizes ideas, visions, and inspiration. Every idea exists first as a thought, image, or feeling. If you honor this inner impulse, you have access to an inexhaustible treasure trove of inspiration. This brings innovation and creativity, and also clarity and perspective.
  You can imagine ether as a kind of invisible funnel through which we receive our ideas and inspiration. The funnel flows through the crown, at the topmost point of the head.

- **Mind corresponds to Element: Air**
  This element represents our analytical mind. It symbolizes planning, organizing, and structure. A person who creates from this area is a very good manager. A clear understanding, paired with holistic linking brings foresight. As we sometimes say: "my head is too full." This expresses the idea that a person can no longer think clearly or formulate structured thoughts. On the physical level, the element Air is associated with the forehead.
- **"Inner Fire" corresponds to Element: Fire**
  This element symbolizes action, the power of inspiration, and man's inner wisdom. It embodies centeredness. A person who lives completely from their center is a calming influence. He radiates calm. This person communicates security. Others feel uplifted and positive in their presence. And a person who is at home on this level is not easily fazed. He remains present with himself and can take people and things simply as they are. As the saying goes: "Through thick and thin" – which means that two people can have such an intimate relationship that they will go through everything together and maintain a deep trust. The element Fire is associated with the heart chakra in the middle of the chest.
- **Emotions correspond to Element: Water**
  This element represents the emotions, depth, flow, and movement. The social competency of a person dwells on this level. People who are active at this level are very sensitive and can empathize strongly with others. They know what those around them need to feel motivated and happy. We speak of "having a sinking feeling" when something feels off. Conflict and stress cause many people stomach problems, if their energy sits in their belly. On the physical level, the element Water is assigned to the abdomen.
- **Body corresponds to Element: Earth**
  The element Earth incorporates structure, order, security, and stability. This level brings pragmatism. If it is healthily balanced with the other elements, it offers a feeling and expres-

sion of self-confidence and self-trust. As we say when we're feeling uncertain: "We lose our footing". On the physical level, the element Earth is associated with the pelvic floor area and the feet.

Tips and Tricks

People who live in synch with their personal rhythm convey a sense of calm and tranquility. They are a rock in the storm. In spite of surrounding hectic and chaos, they can keep a clear head and make smart decisions. Their charisma draws others to them. They have an effect on their surroundings. That is why they are born leaders. The five elements are one of many ways to restore personal balance. They are a path in harmony with nature and with man.

We learn from our mistakes. Some people are only able to grow from personal experience and who want to experience everything firsthand. Personalities like these seldom choose the path of least resistance. But there are also always people who seek out solutions and who want to move forward more easily.

Every project starts with an idea, whether conscious or unconscious. Consciously developed visions give a project a clear direction. A clear vision is crucial. Anyone who wants to skip a few bumps in the rode and maintain motivation throughout the entire process or journey should bear this in mind. It's like with a taxi: if you know where you're going, you'll arrive at your destination. That is why it is important to always ask yourself: What do I want? Where am I going? What is my idea for project X?

You should write down these visions, goals, and actions on a piece of paper. Writing it down is the first step to realize an idea. You should also regularly check your personal goals and visions with your own needs and wishes. Visions and goals have the greatest power when they are wishes of the heart. Centering in your personal middle, in your heart is the key to success. Love attracts love; dismal thoughts attract discouraged and negative people.

If your project does not meet with success, despite a holistic approach (spiritual project management), then it usually is because there is a discrepancy between your heart's desires and the desires of your ego. This circumstance can be recognized and corrected through personal time off and recovery or by a spiritual teacher. Sometimes, however, in spite of all our efforts, we have to admit that it's not time – or not *yet* time – for the project in question. Then we have to let go and consider new options.

Tip: Learn in Harmony with Nature

Nature offers everything that man needs. She can renew herself daily. If a branch is cut off a tree, for example, a new one will soon grow in its place. The way back to nature helps humans deal with stress and performance pressure more calmly. Specific actions will be given through the five elements.

One way to circumvent this performance pressure is to get back to nature. That means to get back to our true personality. If you know who you are, what you can do, and where you want to get to, you can deal with everyday life calmly and serenely, despite the excitement and hectic activity that surrounds you. You will keep a clear head with eyes single-mindedly focused on your personal goals. Moreover, you will effectively and efficiently complete your personal and professional projects.

The five elements symbolize the power that works through nature. They are laws that support and promote the personal processes of change and development. They help people recognize and understand their personalities. And they show us the possible scope of action. The elements are signposts in a terrain that is difficult to comprehend. They offer structure and order and convey security and stability. Ancient mystics knew about this power and used it selectively.

In your work with the five elements, consider your actions per the elements. They will help your processes of change, and development is bound to happen more easily.

Tip: Budget your Strength

In the time of upheaval and rapid change that lies before us, it will be more and more important to budget our resources of strength. Budget carefully. Always take care to recharge yourself with new energy and take strength for your next steps. Take time for yourself, plan "quiet time" into your schedule. The path to stillness through meditation is an option to escape times of hectic for a moment. Chose the option that best matches to you and take time daily for that option. It could be 3 quality minutes, or more. You will see that everything is easier when you do so, and that the time invested in stillness brings a big return.

Tip: The Middle Path

Do you walk the middle path? Your "Inner Fire" is your centering pole. Get to know it and kindle your fire. It will bring you satisfaction, well-being, and happiness.

Bring your masculine and feminine competencies into harmony and live from your middle (Element: Fire). The degree of balance is promising. The time when women needed to be like men to experience professional success is gone. But it's also not the time for men to become like women. Every individual is a unique personality. An invaluable diamond is blazing in your middle, waiting to be rediscovered.

In times of turmoil and change, your personal middle, your "Inner Fire" brings stability and security. It exudes a feeling of belonging in the surrounding cold. It is a place of retreat and stillness. There is always light here, even when darkness threatens without.

This long-time knowledge of meditators in Asia and among original peoples is now offered as a chance for the western world. Diving into this diamond in every person's center brings balance and reduces stress. It is a reliable means to enjoy a healthy, strong, and joyful life.

Tip: Potential Development with the Five Elements

If you want to develop your vision with the five elements, sleep, as well as calm and rest, will help you realize your dreams. All of the other elements and their themes can also be developed through various actions. You can find other variations under: "Suggested actions to Reach Your Goals Easily and Quickly with the Five Elements."

To Do

Come up with actions to reach your goals more quickly and easily. The already mentioned Tips and Tricks will support you in this. Certainly, other possibilities will occur to you. Compare your personal and your spiritual project management.

Procedure:
1. Have you put your vision (Element: Ether) in the first place? If not, your first step is to clarify your vision. Create an image (imaginative or physical) of your personal and professional future.
2. Is your second place occupied with planning (Element: Air) or the element Fire? If so, then combine your power/spirit of action with a good plan in the future. If another element

is in this place, then replace this step with specific written planning. It is important that you can stand behind and carry out your plan.
3. The third position belongs to implementation (Element: Fire). Put Fire here if it is not already there. Give yourself a gentle kick in the pants (mentally). It will help you to realize what you've set out to do.
4. Review your visions and goals regularly. Do they still feel right (Element: Water), or should something change? Water is also the level of teams and partnerships. As a fourth step, ask yourself if the people involved in your project are experiencing win-win situations. Maybe there are people who have a strong influence on you, without being directly involved in your project. Are these relationships profitable and empowering for you? If not, what can you change here? Would talking about it help? If you did not place the element Water in this position, then the above mentioned points are even more important.
5. The element Earth, completion and celebrating, belongs at the end of a project. If it is in another position in your diagram, this usually indicates blockages. Too much grounding blocks. You cannot move forward and are stuck.

Questions for personal reflection:
- Do I have a clear vision and idea of my personal and professional future?
- Are my goals my heart's desires?
- What do I really want?
- Where does my heart pull me?
- What will I do to keep my motivation high during my journey?
- Am I using my energy wisely, so that I can reach my goal?
- Am I doing that which makes me happy and satisfied?

Possible actions to reach your goals more quickly and easily with the five elements:
- **Ether**
Get enough sleep, plan and take time for rest and quiet
- **Air**
Breathe fresh air, practice conscious breathing
- **Fire**
Take the stairs instead of the elevator, go for a walk, get some light exercise such as jogging, biking, or in-line skating, take action, and incorporate a new behavior/habit
- **Water**
Drink pure (e.g., filtered) water or water that has been energized with a Harmonizer, take a bath or shower, detox with nettle tea. (You can purchase the Harmonizer in my online shop at: www.bernardi.li)
- **Earth**
Eat healthily, take dietary supplements, engage in moderate exercise, walk barefoot in nature, and work in the garden

Personal Insights

At the end of this exercise or before you go to bed, take a moment and answer the following questions intuitively:
- What personal insights can I take from this exercise?
- What points will I develop in the future?
- When will I begin to apply these insights?

Find Your Vision – Develop Your Motivational Phrase

Vision finding will help you ingrain the processes introduced in this book. Through this, the permanency of your personal development will be supported. Moreover, this part of the book will give you the foundation you need for effective application in daily life.

The Vision Finding comes from the themes that have revealed themselves through the BERNARDI Profile® tests.

Self-Test: Find Your Vision

Procedure:
- Read again through your insights from the individual exercises and condense the most important themes into a few short, positive sentences. Concentrate on those aspects of each exercise that motivated you. Write these sentences down under Vision Finding in the following table. An example for Point 2, regarding your "Inner Team" could be: I am a holistic personality with strong intuition. I am very sensitive.
- Under "My vision (Motivational Phrase)", condense all these Vision Finding sentences again to one or more cohesive motivational sentences. What is important is that these sentences motivate you effectively. It could be that one key phrase crystalizes for you out of this process, for example: Following the path of the heart.
- If it feels right, assign a color to your motivational phrase. Maybe a symbol also comes to you that supports the phrase. Make a note of the color and symbol.
- Over the next weeks, keep your motivational sentence and symbol near you or hang it up in a place where you will see it often. The bathroom mirror or near your computer screen are good options.

- Make an effort to wear the color that supports your motivational phrase. You can also bring this color into your life with flowers or bath towels. I'm sure you already have an idea how you can integrate it into your daily life.
- Contemplate your motivational phrase and your symbol whenever you are having a tough time. It will remind you of your personal and professional visions and goals and give you strength.
- If you want, integrate your motivational phrase in a meditation before you fall asleep or when you get up in the morning. You can also speak your motivational phrase out loud.

BERNARDI Profile®	Vision Finding
Tree	
Inner Team	
Colors	
Cycles	
Chakras	
Relationship Map	
Shamanic Timeline Trip	
Project Management	

My Vision (Motivational Phrase):

_____
_____
_____
_____
_____

Tips and Tricks

Motivation Meditation

Include your motivational phrase in a meditation before you go to sleep and when you wake up in the morning.

Procedure:
- Assume a comfortable position, sitting or lying down. Turn off all sources of disturbance, e.g., cell phones, telephones, etc., so that you won't be interrupted.
- Close your eyes; inhale and exhale deeply through your nose. Place both hands on your bellybutton. Feel how your belly rises as you inhale and sinks as you exhale. Follow the breath-flow with your thoughts. If other thoughts come up, let them pass through like clouds across the sky. Thoughts come and go. Let them go.
- Follow your breath with your thoughts until you are completely calm. Lay both hands on your heart chakra and concentrate completely on your motivational phrase. You can say it aloud or silently a few times.

Mantra

Repeat your motivational phrase often. Ideally, it includes the phrase "I Am". Because whatever you already are, you no longer need to become. You are it. The statement "I Am" kindles your heart flame, the power of your heart.

To Do

Come up with actions to reach your visions more quickly and easily. The Tips and Tricks listed above will help you. You will certainly think of a few other things, as well.

Questions for personal reflection:
1. How can incorporate my motivational phrase more fully in my day? Maybe you could assign a color to your phrase and paint a picture with this color. Hang this picture somewhere you will see it often.
2. Review your motivational phrase after 2–3 weeks. Has the phrase changed? Should something be added to it or taken away?

Personal Insights

At the end of this exercise or before you go to bed, take a moment and answer the following questions intuitively:
- What personal insights can I take from this exercise?
- What points will I develop in the future?
- When will I begin to apply these insights?

Seeking Your Vision – Develop a Vision for all Aspects of Your Life

Do you have a clear vision and a goal for your future? Do you regularly write these down? Every six to twelve months is best. You should write or draw your visions and goals on a piece of paper. This creates commitment and keeps them fresh in your memory. This is the first step to a tangible realization of your desires and needs.

Self-Test: Seeking Your Vision

Procedure:
- Think about your visions and goals in every area of your life.
- Think of simple and applicable actions that you can take to move closer to your dreams.
- Think about which area of your life is most important at present. Prioritize and begin today to apply your list of actions in this area.

Areas	Visions/Goals	Conditions
Career Development		
(Continuing) Education/ Development of Strengths		
Financial/Material Needs		
Spiritual Needs		
Health/Physical Needs		
Partnership		
Family/Children		
Friends		
Other Needs		

Tips and Tricks

Tip: Brainstorming

Develop your visions and goals in a quiet moment when you are open and motivated. Just let your ideas flow. Write down whatever comes to you. Later, you can read back through and decide what really resonates with you.

EXERCISE: Eagle Eye

Albert Einstein said: "We cannot solve our problems with the same thinking we used when we created them." That is why it can be worthwhile to adopt a bird's eye perspective. You can complete this exercise in your thoughts or directly in nature. Go outside and follow a falcon or eagle with your mind's eye. Try to put yourself on his level and immerse yourself in his "being". Soar in the air and observe your goal from far away. How does it look from here?

EXERCISE: Invite the Not-Yet-Realized

Invite the dreams and goals into your life that have not yet been realized. Say silently: I invite Love and Peace in my home. Love and Peace now rule in my home.

Tip: Change of Perspective

Because many people still live in duality, they can decide in every second to see the Good. Commit yourself NOW to your happiness and the fulfillment of your goals. You can also decide to live in love and unity (i.e., on a higher plane, where unity, not duality reigns) at any moment.

Tip: Time

Some goals just take a little bit longer. Also bear in mind that every person has their own rhythm. Some people need longer and others move more quickly. Take that into consideration when you plan.

To Do

Come up with a list of actions to reach your visions more quickly and easily. The Tips and Tricks listed above will help you. You will certainly think of a few other things, as well.

Questions for personal reflection:
1. Do my visions and goals reflect my heart's deepest desires?
2. Is there something deeper behind the desires I have written down? For example, maybe you wish for less stress at home, but the deeper wish behind it is for quiet and rest. The wish behind the wish – that is your true heart's desire. Follow this with all your strength. Make space for it in your life.
3. Review your visions and goals from time to time. Add to and change them whenever they no longer feel right.

Personal Insights

At the end of this exercise or before you go to bed, take a moment and answer the following questions intuitively:
- What personal insights can I take from this exercise?
- What points will I develop in the future?
- When will I begin to apply these insights?

Goal Programming – Begin Realization

Do you want to be more relaxed yet still keep your personal and professional goals in view? The following exercise will help you with this. Goal Programming both relaxes and programs your subconscious for success.

Because the human brain cannot distinguish between reality and imagination, for the brain, imagining becomes reality. Goal Programming builds on this knowledge. It works with the power of thought. In your imagination, your personal goals will be experienced as if they already were achieved. In this way, subconscious mechanisms are set in play that will support you in reaching your personal goals.

Procedure:
1. Assume a comfortable position, sitting or lying down. Turn off all sources of disturbance, e.g., cell phones, telephones, etc., so that you won't be interrupted.
2. Close your eyes; inhale and exhale deeply through your nose. Place both hands on your bellybutton. Feel how your belly rises as you inhale and sinks as you exhale. Follow the breathflow with your thoughts. If other thoughts come up, let them pass through like clouds across the sky. Thoughts come and go. Let them go.
3. Follow your breath flow with your thoughts until you have relaxed. Imagine yourself in a situation that you will soon encounter and that you would like to influence. It could be a meeting with important clients, or an interview, or an afternoon with your sweetheart. Imagine the situation as you would like it to be. Watch this film with your inner eye. What does your goal look like in all its facets? Bring your feelings into the exercise. How do you feel in this situation? How are you doing? What does success feel like in your body? You are the director of your film. Visualize this as long as you like.

4. If you have trouble imagining in images, then complete the Goal Programming with your thoughts. You can tell yourself, for example: I am successful, I am confident, and I trust myself. Put your entire goal into words. It is important that the words be motivating. Avoid negative formulations. As with the imaging, incorporate your feelings. Imagine how you will feel when you have reached your goal. How do you feel? What does success feel like in your body?
5. Take a few deep breaths. Open your eyes and become aware of your physical body and your surroundings.
6. Stand up and physically take a step towards your goal. Imagine you are walking towards your goal. Remain a moment at that point where you imagine your end-goal to be. Consciously experience the power of this space. Feel the joy of accomplishing your goal.

Depending on how active the right half of your brain is, you might not be able to draw up any images with your eyes closed. The exercise still works, however, if you just think the thoughts. With time and practice, the right side of your brain will become more productive.

WHAT ELSE CAN I LET GO OF?

How are your energy reserves? Are you feeling balanced? Do you still have blockages? What themes can be released now? Which ones cannot? The following exercise brings answers to these questions. You will gain strength for daily application through the energy balancing described in this book. Moreover, this closing reflection will help anchor the processes introduced in this book. Using a release ritual, you will be able to let go of the last ballast keeping you from reaching your goals.

EXERCISE: Mind

What ideas are spinning in your mind? Which ones can you let go of? What do you need in order to find joy in your actions?

EXERCISE: Emotions

Is there something that is weighing on you emotionally? It could be a fight with a colleague or a comment from a stranger in the supermarket. If you are present enough with yourself, other people's emotions remain with them. They don't affect you. If something has managed to stick with you, however, let it go. Give these themes a bit of space by accepting the emotions as they are. Draw the emotions into your heart chakra so that they can be transformed and released. Then let it go. Love works everywhere, all the time. Let yourself heal. Let it be healed.

EXERCISE: Heart Chakra

Do something every day that brings you joy. It will do wonders. Do you know what makes you really happy? Allow yourself this joy as often as possible. You are worth it. Take time and make space for your heart's desires. They are the seeds for happy moments and a satisfied life. Live your life as you want it to be now. It is worth it. You are worth it.

Energies – Summon Up Strength for Action

"Everything is energy." Albert Einstein knew (and said) this. We come here as etheric beings, angels and Buddhas, and depart this world as such. In the intervening time, it is balsam for our soul when we remember who we are and what we have committed to do on this earth.

Children are angels with wings. Let your wings also grow again and keep your feet on the ground. Know that, with your thoughts, words, and emotions, you create your world yourself. Be like children. Let things, people, and circumstance pass by you every second without judgement. Stay centered in your heart chakra. Simply be.

Think about it: Every thought produces energy. Send out thoughts of love, to heal yourself and your surroundings.

EXERCISE: Strengthen Your Heart Energetically

Close your eyes and lay your hands on your chest. Draw your thoughts down into the point in the middle of your chest. Focus your attention for a moment on the warmth that your hands radiate into your chest. Maybe you can also feel the energy emanating from your heart chakra. Breathe deeply in and out and open your eyes after a few minutes. Stay as long in this center of love and peace as feels right for you. Enjoy it. Feel yourself.

EXERCISE: Drop Other People's Issues and Problems

Imagine other people's issues like rays of energy that stream horizontally, like radio waves. The divine frequencies come straight down from the Source of all being. You can tune yourself to the frequency that is right for you. Consciously change your channel from the horizontal to the divine frequencies. Stand under the light-shower of pure vibration by imagining a heavenly shower of light above you. Let yourself be cleansed and feed on the pure, clear energy.

Tip: Follow Your Life-flow

Every person's aura is their map. All the emotions, thoughts, and feelings, everything that we are, were, or will be is recorded there. You will become what you are meant to be, if you want to. We have 99.9% free agency. The .1% is the responsibility of the spirit world, which shakes us up if we stray too far from our path. But even then, you have the freedom to remain on your chosen path.

If a person is doing what he committed to do for himself and his life, then things come relatively easily. So let yourself be guided by the impulses of your heart. Trust that it is your heart's path, full of love and miracles. Let it flow. It is beautiful.

Tip: Like Attracts Like

Our auras need to be kept pure. The issues that will come up in the next years want to be released. It is a time of release.

We draw themes, situations, and other people into our lives through our aura, our charisma. If you are advancing more quickly than your environment, it could be that certain things and people no longer match to you. That is why you should divide them into the following categories:
1. People who are important to me and with whom I spend the necessary time so that we are on the same level. It is important that a person who has made a first step continues on their path. You should not stand still because others are not coming with you. Each of us has our own path.

2. People that I will allow to go out of my life. Constantly re-examine your decisions. Time moves quickly. It could be that you change your mind tomorrow. Sometimes people around you take steps that you never thought possible. Bear in mind that some people come into your life as companions for a time, but when their purpose is complete, they will move on. Let them go and be thankful for the hours and experiences shared.

Tip: Law of Attraction

The Law of Attraction says that we attract what we send out, like a magnet. If a person radiates pure love, then he will attract loving people and people who are longing for love. Be mindful of your words, thoughts, and actions. Send out what you wish to receive and you will receive it, if it is your heart's desire.

EXERCISE: Let the Sun In

Change needs energy so that you can take the spiritual and physical steps. Because knowledge only becomes wisdom if it is lived. Look at what your environment is showing you and take the steps necessary to change. Ask your spiritual helpers/the Light-master for help. They will be happy to help.

Go out in nature and turn your face to the sun. Open your chest area by stretching your arms out to the sides. With your eyes open, draw the rays of the sun into your heart chakra. Spread them throughout your entire body. Do this exercise as long as it feels right.

Tip: Fill Up on Strength

If you want to fill up on strength, you need space and opportunity to do so. Since the dawn of time, people have known that everything radiates energy. There are power centers on this earth that emit energy. With energetic Feng Shui, as I teach it in my spiritual coaching course, you can also create a power center from your home. The energy of "power centers" can also be measured. In Switzerland, there are many famous places, such as the monastery chapel in Einsiedeln. Your country also has some power centers. You can find more information about this in books from bookstores near you.

It is worthwhile to take stock of your environment every now and then.

The following questions will help you find some perspective:
- What gives you energy and where do you lose it? Exhilarating moments bring strength. Your rational mind tries to convince you with your thoughts that you have more or less energy; but if you are in the divine Flow, nothing can sap your energy.
- Do you think positive thoughts? There are many who stand in their own way with their thinking. Use the power of your thoughts. Think positively. The power of your thoughts and the advantage this potential brings is a key to your success.
- Do you wear clothing that strengthens you? Friendly, bright colors (like yellow) cheer. Black, depending on the cultural context, diminishes. Take the self-test to see how you react to colors.
- What is your sleep like? Do you wake feeling refreshed and rested? There are symbols (such as the Harmonizer in my shop: www.bernardi.li) that can harmonize your room.
- Do you sometimes have headaches? Headaches can come from tension in the neck and back. There are also people who react with headaches to artificial additives in food (E-numbers), wheat, or other food products. Pay attention to your body's signals. They will show you what is good for you.

EXERCISE: Strengthen Your Personality

1. Release past themes: Let lightness enter into your life. Imagine that you are packing up everything you want to release in stones. You can say: "I fill the stones in my hands with all the themes that I can release now. All the issues that I am ready to let go of flow into these stones." Then imagine you throw them away. You can also do this exercise with real stones. Maybe you will need to do the exercise a few times until you really feel light. You can also release extra body weight with this exercise and say goodbye to those pounds. Repeat this exercise every day, until you feel light on your feet.
2. Connect with nature: Take a walk outside. Look around you and appreciate the nature you see. Really see the green of the grass or the white of the snow. Stop for a moment and sense the energy that the nature around you gives you. You can fill up your batteries with the energy of the trees and fields. Your energy field, your aura, will be strengthened. Your charisma will radiate beautifully.
3. Flying high: Open yourself to the heaven above you by observing the starry night sky. Consciously make contact with the stars, the moon, or the blue of the sky. Imagine that your batteries are recharging. Fill up on the power of the starry sky. Draw the power of the stars, the moon, or the blue sky into your physical body. You can also do this exercise with the sun.
4. Thankfulness: Take a quiet moment to think of all the things you are thankful for. What can you be proud of? What have you already achieved? Speak your words of thanksgiving aloud or in your heart. Feel the thankfulness in your heart chakra. Practice thankfulness every day.

EXERCISE: Staying Present

In order to fully experience your potential and your innate abilities, it is crucial that you stay present with yourself. Breathe deliberately into your heart chakra and your forehead. Breathe deeply and feel deeply into your heart chakra and then into your forehead as you inhale.

Tip: Release

Letting go is worth it. When you do, you make room for something new. Just like a new outfit needs space in your closet, energy in your life also needs its space.
One way to release is to forgive by forgiving everything. Use the Law of Forgiveness for people, circumstances, and everything that you want to come to terms with. You can do this exercise over and over. Whenever you feel that you want to feel free. You can be free of circumstances, people, and your past. Live and enjoy freedom here on earth.
   Be aware that hostility and anger bind. Free yourself from these emotions so that you are free to be what you really are. So practice forgiveness.
Another way to release is through conscious breathing. With every inhale, you receive new energy and inspiration. With every exhale, you release everything heavy and burdensome.

EXERCISE: Cord Cutting

Imagine or draw two circles on a paper. You stand in one circle. The person or situation from which you wish to be released is in the other. Draw a golden wall between the two circles so that each has its own space.

Tip: Release What Doesn't Belong to You

When people are present with themselves and their field is stable, then energy from other people such as envy and jealousy doesn't have a chance. The person's aura is inviolable. They stay present with their own energy, regardless of what is happening around them.

If you notice that you are not totally present with yourself then let everything that is not yours flow out of your body through your right hand and draw your energy back to you through your left.

Tip: Light-water

Spraying light-water and placing rice with Himalayan salt and halite (for grounding) in three corners of a room will clean the space. The atmosphere stays pure and clear. The rice should be placed so that two bowls are near a window or a door. Only fill the rice bowls (or glasses) half-way full.

Tip: Bless

Blessings radiates a wonderful energy and works wonders. Gift light. Bless everything you encounter so that the world will be flooded with God's pure light. I personally use the Merkaba blessing. It stands for peace in heaven and on earth, since it incorporates two peace symbols. One symbol points down to earth and the other upwards to heaven.

You can offer this blessing in your heart or use your finger or an incense stick. The Merkaba blessing is as follows:
1. I bless you
2. In
3. Love
4. Surround you with light (start above and circle clockwise)

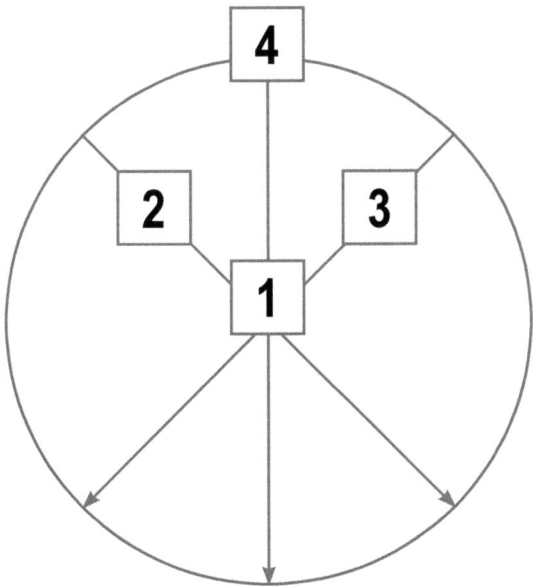

Tip: Connection with the Divine

Connect with the highest Source, with God in heaven and with the heart of Mother Earth. Let the love and light of heaven and earth stream through you. Radiate love from your heart like a sun. This is healing for you and the world.

Tip: Live Heart-Consciousness

Focus your energy on what is important for you. Create space in your life for new and inspiring things by opening your heart chakra. Live from you heart. Fully enjoy what you do. Every moment is unique. A new moment is beginning now.

Reflection – Keep it Going

You have almost reached the end of the book. You can live your life more and more every day. Live what makes you happy. Let go. In order to continue to develop even more lightly and buoyantly, reflect on these questions in a quiet moment:
1. What personal insights have I drawn from the exercises in this book?
2. What points will I continue to practice in the future:
3. When will I apply these insights to my life?
4. Do I need something else to continue my development? If yes, what and how will I bring it into my life?
5. Is there someone who can support me as I apply these things to my life?

Releasing Ritual – Release the Final Baggage

1. You can do the Detachment Meditation with eyes open or closed. Assume a comfortable position. Inhale and exhale deeply through your nose. Let your breath come and go.
2. Concentrate completely on the issue that is presently weighing on you or that you want to release. Name the issue, for example, "yucky feeling in stomach", "stress with my friend", "impatience".
3. Tell yourself: I enclose issue X (repeat its name) and everything that belongs to it in my heart chakra.
4. Fill the issue in your heart chakra with your love by radiating from your heart like a love-sun.
5. If you want, you can add the following sentence: I allow everything that is not mine to flow from my body.

Some things are easy to release; others need some time. It can happen that an issue will return in another facet. If so, you should repeat the exercise.

CLOSING REMARKS

I want to thank my youngest daughter for her inspiration. She supported me during my pregnancy with the writing of this book through her pure and clear energy. I would also like to thank my other two daughters. You are a life's mission that is always beautiful, challenging, and inspiring. You imprint life with the future. I love you.

Thank you to my spiritual helpers and guides, who always support me. A shaman once said to me: God has good things for you. Yes, God has good things for everyone, when we align ourselves with this Source.

I wish for you, dear Reader, strength and courage to tread your heart's path and to follow your visions. You are unique and can be true to who you are. Let yourself be you.

Finally, I would like to thank my dear "Mami" for her support in the background, and sometimes on the front lines. You are the best Mommy in the world. Thank you for everything.

And my grandfather, Bababa, who has always stood by me whenever I need support. Thank you so much, with all my heart.

I thank all the people who have supported and accompanied me, consciously and unconsciously with all my heart. I have so many loving people around me. Thank you all for being there. I love you all.

LARA BERNARDI

After completing her studies in Business Economics and a career in the business world, Lara Bernardi dedicated herself completely to her assignment as a spiritual teacher. Lara guides people to their creator-consciousness and to uncover riches on earth.

Lara Bernardi is a business economist FH, spiritual teacher, and mother of three girls. She has written numerous specialist articles for business magazines and is the author of several books and a meditation CD. Lara is a fully integrated personality who follows the Path of the Heart (Love) and consciousness. As a spiritual teacher, she counsels holistically using her clear-sightedness and clarity.

Since childhood, she has been conscious of the immaterial realms and was already lead by her divine guide, the I AM in her heart. The divine voice in her was, and is, her regular companion. For

Lara, there is no difference between the subtle and the material. She has the ability to perceive people on all levels. Because of this, she can clearly reveal to them where their potential and possibilities lie. She sees, feels, and understands energies. This allows her to advise her clients in all areas. Lara has the talent to understand people holistically and to show them who they are and what they can do in order to live the richest possible kind of life.

Using her years of practical coaching experience, Lara developed the BERNARDI Profile® as an assessment of personality and individual potential.

Lara offers training in mediumship, spiritual counseling, and new methods of healing as well as numerous seminars on how to become happy and healthy and how to make contact with the light-masters. Lara guides people to their I Am in their heart chakra, so that they can realize their true beings and live their potential on earth.

It is Lara's goal to unite heaven on earth with consciousness and love so that it is possible to be happy. Loka samasta sukhino bhavantu.

You can find more information on Lara Bernardi, her seminars, and products at: www.bernardi.li.

novum PUBLISHER FOR NEW AUTHORS

The publisher

He who stops being better stops being good.

This is the motto of novum publishing, and our focus is on finding new manuscripts, publishing them and offering long-term support to the authors.
Our publishing house was founded in 1997, and since then it has become THE expert for new authors and has won numerous awards.

Our editorial team will peruse each manuscript within a few weeks free of charge and without obligation.

You will find more information about
novum publishing and our books on the internet:

www.novum-publishing.co.uk

Lara Bernardi

The Key to Happiness

ISBN 978-3-99048-516-3
100 Seiten

Your heart can provide you with all the power you need to make your goals and wishes a reality. Use it! This book leads you through a process for harnessing the energies of consciousness and love that will allow you to become the architect of your own life.

Lara Bernardi

The Key to Health

ISBN 978-3-99048-667-2
104 Seiten

Find new opportunities, strength, and motivation. Your body can regenerate completely naturally. Your health is the foundation and basis for a happy self. Strengthen your health and stimulate your powers of self-healing!

Rate this book on our website!

www.novum-publishing.co.uk